BECOMING

as

GOD INTENDED

Bruce E. Metzger

WestBow
PRESS®
A DIVISION OF THOMAS NELSON
& ZONDERVAN

WestBow Press books may be ordered through booksellers or by contacting:

WestBow Press
A Division of Thomas Nelson & Zondervan
1663 Liberty Drive
Bloomington, IN 47403
www.westbowpress.com
1 (866) 928-1240

ISBN: 978-1-9736-1129-5 (sc)
ISBN: 978-1-9736-1130-1 (hc)
ISBN: 978-1-9736-1128-8 (e)

Library of Congress Control Number: 2017919217

Print information available on the last page.

WestBow Press rev. date: 1/4/2018

For Camille, I miss you even when I am with you. At times,
you overlooked when I was away from you, so I could write.

Opening Quotes

How old would you be if you did not know your age? . . . One of the advantages of growing up is that no one tells you anymore that you are too smart for your own good. The days when your intelligence used you get you into trouble are over. You among your peers at long last and everyone is at least as cleaver as you are. In such company, men can stop being dense and women don't have to be coy any longer.

Véronique Vienna, *The Art of Growing Up*,
Clarkson Potter Publishers, pp. 8, 36.

The soul is empty. It is a bucket, not a geyser. The soul is made to want. This is not due to sin. It is aggravated by sin. Our spiritual vulnerability, our spiritual neediness, our emptiness is built-in, hard-wired, standard circuitry. The essence of sin is the desire to live without God, to be subsistent, to be invulnerable.

David Hansen, *A Little Handbook on Having A Soul*, InterVarsity Press, p. 42.

Wisdom in its broadest and commonest sense denotes sound and serene judgment regarding the conduct of life. It may be accompanied by a broad range of knowledge, by intellectual acuteness, and by speculative depth, but it is not to be identified with any of these and may appear in their absence. It involves intellectual grasp or insight, but it is concerned not so much with the ascertainment of fact or the elaboration of theories as with ends of practical life.

Brand Blanshard, *The Encyclopedia of Philosophy*
Macmillian Publishing Co, Vol 8, p. 324.

If you want your life not to stray too far from your soul, you need to make tiny adjustments so that from your line of action does not go off at a tangent from the circle of the soul. In these constant adjustments by which we try to keep soul and body in touch, we are much like the sailor with his hand on the tiller, correcting course, now this side, now that, all day long. The sailor knows he is never quite on course, always a little off, always in need of small adjustments.

Correcting course all day long: This is the beginning of wisdom. It is a practice, a quiet noticing of where you actually are, not being right on, but slightly off. The Greek word *Sophia* ("philosophy," love of wisdom), originally means the skill in a craft such as the helmsman. The wisdom of the body keeps its alignment with the soul by noticing when they diverge.

James Hillman, *The Force of Character*, Random House, pp. 127-8.

The spiritual life is not abstract. It thrives on ritual, art, good works, and symbolic acts. These concrete actions bring transition home physically, emotionally, and intellectually. In this way, you know you have gone through a change, and you can adjust accordingly.

Thomas Moore, *Dark Nights of the Soul*, Gotham Books, p. 34.

The Christian faith is the discovery of that center in God who sticks with us, the righteous God. Christian discipleship is a decision to walk in his ways, steadily and firmly, and then finding that the way interests all our interests, passions and gifts, our human needs and our eternal aspirations.

Eugene Peterson, *A Long Obedience In The Same Direction*, InterVarsity Press, p. 134.

By God, I mean a being absolutely infinite – that is, a substance consisting in infinite attributes, of which each expresses eternal and infinite essentiality. *Explanation.* – I say absolutely infinite, not infinite after its kind: for, of a thing infinite only after its kind, infinite attributes may be denied; but that which is absolutely infinite, contains in its essence whatever expresses reality, and involves no negation.

Benedict (Baruch) De Spinoza, The Philosophy of
Benedict De Spinoza, Tubor Publishing, p. 39.

The art of being wise is the art of knowing what to overlook.

William James, editor E. P. Aldrich,
As Willian James Said, Vanguard Press, p.62.

Contents

Introduction 1

Open Here 5

Christian Spirituality 13

Get Personal 33

Born to Become 49

Words Are Power Tools 65

Deal with It 75

Deal with It, Again 95

Be Someone, It Takes Faith, Trouble, Temptation. 119

This Thing Called Faith 137

Close Here: Towards a Future 147

Random Thoughts 173

Aftereffect 187

Bibliography 209

Index 211

INTRODUCTION

More than likely, on a subconscious level we are aware that ideas shape our spirituality and not only our intellectuality. I have gleaned from the Bible and other philosophical and theological ideas, with a slight dance around some psychological associated ideas that make my spiritual autobiography. Reaching into my Christian spiritual experiences with ideas connected to that growing experience. Some Believers will be able to identify with the ideas presented. Those that do not have an immediate identification, you are invited to discover viable ideas that are at home with Christian spirituality and human nature. Ideas shape who we can be as a person. Experience *brings* familiarity. There is recognition, as much as possible, what is familiar can be trusted.

The ideas that shaped my spirituality are mostly from the Bible. So, there are more than a few biblical references cited. Those people who tend to be less confrontational, say it is wise to avoid getting into arguments, including polite discussions over religion and politics. To exclude the psychological condition – some of us throw out from a distance, an analysis of people we do not know nor have a connection to them. If the claim is we cannot analyse correctly, however, from a distance, the accuracy will be less reliable or worthy; it will be surface at best. Nevertheless, avoidance of religious subjects and political leanings, do not help us to understand people and life. Is that all there is to people and life – religion and politics with a mixed bag of psychological analysis? People are more than various psychological labels. All of us have meaning through spirituality, of some sort. That is experienced in the arena of the personal life and the reality where politics has a life of its own, brings some zigzag moments. In spite of such other loose-ended influences for spiritual implications, the crucial influence in my life has been and still is Christian spirituality

The ideas presented here mean a lot. They have depths that sprout meaning that has changed my life. The intent is that some of the ideas will have the effect as seeds planted to grow some deeper meaning to life with the personal sense of self as the new self, generated from salvation. Good probing ideas can cause anyone to experience God and their own new self, somewhat more profound than before. That experience with God and the self is a direct connection to growth that reaches deep within the soul. All of us have that inherent need to understand our spiritual way of being, with the inclusion of intellectual satisfaction. We experience spiritual growing pains however, slightly different from each other, yet always personal because we begin to grow from unique and with varying intellectual abilities and style. Each of us has a philosophical temperament, which is an aspect of the nature of human nature.

As human beings, each one of us does not live simply as material objects. Is the corporeal body that much of a nuisance to be without a sense of spirituality? The sense of being spiritual is the means to look at reality as spiritually minded but at peace with our material body. That seems reasonable and positive when there is intellectual substance to our spirituality. The Bible encourages the Believer and the wannabe Believer, to experience a depth of spirituality so that intellectually such a spirituality is a practice living an authentic life, not just ideas stuffed in the head. What that experience and practice looks like is a satisfaction with our own personality but which also pleases the Lord Jesus. We become the person God has intended for us to be.

The *becoming* part of who or what we are as a person has the effect to reach into every aspects of our life. How we live our Christian spirituality, gets us into the tall grass where discernment seems out of sight and nuances lurk around the intellectual corners. Not one person, who claims to be a Christian, can experience the depth of Christian spirituality solely by intellectual acknowledgement by itself, alone, without some reasonable ideas from biblical concepts and by what other Believers have to think about such concepts. No doubt, even a simple, uncomplicated, belief in God, is not a gamble of chance, played like solitaire. Christians have an identifiable relationship with other Christians on a spiritual level and on a material level; connections are personal with depth of authenticity, experienced in daily life. Should there be any solitaire lone wolfs as Christians? No. We Christians are a family, even if we do not like to admit it. Not every Christian within the spiritual family is up to speed on understanding the importance what it means to *become* more than what they were before. However, absolutely, that indicates every one of us in this spiritual family, either grows at different grades and each one has begun their spiritual life at different times. Spiritual growth may seek similar results of improvements in personality and how life is lived, however at its hub it is highly subjective, because we all grow from where we initially are at as an individual. Wisdom and patience is required.

Bible quotations are primarily a base, jumping off point. The primary biblical source is the *New Century Version* (NCV) and secondary source the *English Standard Version* (ESV). The words "Believer" and "Christian" are interchangeable, as it seems natural. The references to "Jesus" usually has the additional name "Christ," which is not necessarily be applied, although Jesus is meant to infer that, since Jesus is the "Christ" the Savior. "Jesus" in the Bible, is identified as "Jesus Christ," other instances as "Christ Jesus." Besides, the New Testament uses "Jesus" more often probably for social custom. We do the same today; refer to someone either by their first name or by given name and people know who it is. Certain people, however, known by a single name, are a mononym. Besides, the name "Jesus" cuts to the nub. The accustomed mononyms for example, are brainiacs as Socrates, Voltaire, and Nietzsche with musicians as Enya, Moby, and Sting. Such a short list, with a host of other luminaries and infamous tyrants, are unlimited. While reading, some may detect a slight playfulness in the grammatical structure. It is an attempt to curb sarcasm.

What follows are numbered statements of personal conclusions and affirmations. They are an account of concepts and beliefs that shaped my life and my thinking, to date. These statements satisfy my philosophical temperament where questions have been answered about my spiritual longings, to date. To refer the numbered statements as aphorisms might be a stretch, although some are short and pithy. Within each chapter, the numbered statements of conclusions and affirmations are not necessarily built upon the pervious numbered section. They are gleaned from my experiences, learning, and education. The preferred older English, pronoun style such as *they, them, their,* is used instead the awkward his/her. The older method seems not infested with political correctness and prevents "grammatical whiplash" (grammergirl.com).

OPEN HERE

1

To grow spiritually has its own problems. Spiritual growth pays attention to heartaches. These heartaches are either about knowing too little or knowing too much. Knowing too little is the cause for an ineffective practice on how to live with less existential troubles. However, for the person who knows too much, they live too much in their head because the choice is much broader as to know how to act. Authentic spiritual growth should not bring paralysis.

2

Christians live simultaneously in two worlds, juxtaposed, yet dealing with what consists of evil and good forces. Meandering between these forces are some questionable problem gray areas. Wisdom is required.

3

Christians live with the expectation that they can be spiritually minded. Christians are able to think cogently and with intelligence about the reality of spirituality. To be spiritually minded therefore means to consider the totality of reality. The material reality is not everything, on its surface. There's more going on than meets the eye.

4

The feeling of impotency, that nothing can be done to stand against evil, against the discrepancies and oddball contradictions that seem to pour out from evil and from ordinary events, causes the good to be oblivious, to what is going on before the eyeballs. So far, that is normal reality. That contrast, jolts, every time the thought floats to the surface of consciousness. Indifference is evil about the good.

5

It is not an exaggeration when Paul an apostle, opines for the spiritually minded Christian, "Our fight is not against people on earth but against rulers and authorities and powers of this world's darkness, against the spiritual powers of evil in the heavenly world."[1] That is conditional however, since he tells us in verse 11, that the spiritually minded are those who have protection ("armor") from God to deal with the "devil's evil tricks." We deal with what is behind what is facing us.

Where does the good come from? Does the good come from anything, of its own accord? According to James, the good comes from God. He says, "Every good action and every perfect gift is from God."[2] However, previously, James informs that, "Evil cannot tempt God, and God himself does not tempt anyone."[3] We can be tempted, as humans, by inordinate desires as it clearly states, "But people are tempted when their own evil desire leads them away and traps them. This desire leads to sin, and then the sin leads to death."[4] Evil shows up where the good is absent – usually. Do not suppose therefore that

---

[1] NCV, Ephesians 6: 12.
[2] NCV, James 1: 17.
[3] NCV, James 1: 13.
[4] NCV, James 1: 14, 15.

evil is not a creative force to destroy our freedom, in any moment. Indifference to evil is a skillful ability to embrace ignorance as a bliss.

6

The person who has been made new through the salvation experience brings with it a newness which means to be changed, different, more advanced from being a mere individual somebody, just like everyone else, who has, however, become authentic and is viewed as a someone for whom God has intended for them to be. The new spiritual self of identity, as experienced in the newness of being alive spiritually is not bound, held captive, to the shame of past sins. Believers live with an innocent blush.

We can agree with Paul an apostle, when he says, "I want them to be strengthened and joined together with love so that they may be rich in their understanding. This leads to their knowing fully God's perfect secret, that is, Christ himself. In him all treasures of wisdom and knowledge are safely kept."[5] God may keep treasures of wisdom and knowledge, but it is to our interest and advantage to find them and bring out from their depths, insights to live by. God is not willing to spoon-feed us. Learning and reading opens the soul to God's ideas.

7

Becoming the person God wants for each of us to be, is an on-going process and better achieved by learning and growing, becoming, as it is pointed out, "by a new way of thinking."[6] Acquiring a new way of thinking and understanding about reality and our own self, especially as a new redeemed self, takes patience, time, and a whole lot of forgiveness towards our own sense as a person.

---

[5] NCV, Colossians 2: 2, 3.
[6] NCV, Romans 12: 2.

8

Paul reveals the skinny on what is going on within Christianity. Averred directly that for those who have grown spiritually: "Then you can be filled with the fullness of God,"[7] Paul adds. Apparently, not all Believers have that "fullness." It takes some intellectual nudging now and then to grow spiritually. This means the Believer has some say or input on *how* they are growing spiritually. What does not mix well is Christian spirituality and intellectual laziness. Because this spirituality seeks completion, depth that feels full, with a peace that satisfies. It is not complicated.

9

The Christian life can be lived reasonably and in a practical manner. Simply put, it must be lived reasonably and in a practical manner. However, often along the way, the Believer can become unreasonable or excessively irksome and vain, too neatly packaged and tiresome. Such a Believer becomes a boring pedantic and not practical. What is, moreover, unreasonable is that the boring pedantic has the stench of self-righteousness. The boring pedantic knows enough, however with little understanding, but certainly no wisdom. They are able to describe Christian spirituality, but not capable to explain the nuances that are embedded in spiritual growth. The practical is lost on the boring pedantic. Every Believer should become long in the tooth, which means they can be reasonable and practical and wise.

10

Those that are spiritually enlightened can frequently give off the stench of self-righteousness. All of us have given off that odour, when we are honest.

---

[7] NCV, Ephesians 3: 19, context vs.14-19. See 4: 13, ESV, "fullness of Christ."

11

The Christian should never feel inferior! They should not be inferior, less than what God has begun to accomplish in their personal life, deep in the soul or self. Regardless of the degree, the Christian has matured spiritually and intellectually; it is the Christian's condition of being. There should never be a situation that allows criticisms or words used to belittle the extent Christian's advancements in their spiritual growth. Every Christian should always think – since they are growing – of themselves as more spiritually mature than what they were before. Confidence first, then humility, but both are required.

12

When we are in the presence of a mature Christian and can sense their spiritual depth, it simply feels good. It is a feel and a knowing, as though we are exactly where we should be. That presence, sense, and depth, is the power of the Holy Spirit and the authenticity that emanates from the mature Christian's personality.

13

We need the theoretical as much as the practical. The theoretical provides working knowledge, so that we are not high and dry not knowing how to think, what to be as a person. Theoretical ideas give speculation to cogitate and determine if ideas can be practically lived as a pleasing life, which also please ourselves.

14

The spiritual life involves a learning curve. Initially, simply believing is a form of unthinking acceptance of the experience of spirituality. All those who want to believe with further depth and authenticity must acquire intelligible ideas. Simply believing is not enough, however a good place to begin. It is not practical for spiritual growth to be understood in a less effective way. The Christian has to understand the difference from their *then* experience by knowing what is *now*, so that they can know where they are going spiritually. Christian spirituality, therefore, is not about soft, fluffy, easy ideas that abandons experiences or blindly follows groupthink. That would be spiritual death, or, be intellectually lazy and a bit crazy in an off sort of way. The learning curve is always curving.

15

Do you recall the exciting drama surrounding the story[8] of the woman who washes Jesus feet? This nameless woman does not wash with water from the owner's house, but from her own tears. She also has a bottle of perfume. The owner of the residence is a Pharisee teacher, named Simon. The woman dries the feet of Jesus with her long sexy hair. Not to stop there, she kisses his feet, then sprinkles perfume on the feet of Jesus. According to the storyline, her reputation is the local loose woman in town. There always seems to be a loose woman in most towns. The religious teacher himself however, made the accusation, if Jesus is whom he claims, then Jesus would catch on as to the woman's character. Simon knew her, sort of. How did he know the woman? She was the woman to talk about, right? Jesus also knew what sort of person the nameless woman was all about, (verse 47 hints to that). Luke gives this account told about Jesus and the unnamed woman who sprinkled perfume on his feet (verse 46). We do not know how much perfume she poured out. However, consider the expense of the perfume, perhaps very little.

From the account given by John[9], we have a similar story about perfume and Jesus feet. This time the woman has a name, and her

[8] NCV, Luke 7: 36-50.
[9] NCV, John 12: 1-11.

name is Mary. Mary does not cry over the feet of Jesus. This story takes place among friends and another good meal. The story gets a bit confusing. Matthew[10] writes while Jesus has a meal, perfume was poured on the head of Jesus not his feet. That means not too much perfume was poured out, although it had a potent and pleasant aroma. What we have is two different stories, with two different women and the story with Mary is the named woman. Twice, Mary is mentioned. What causes confusion between the narratives, the Pharisee's name is Simon (verse 40) and the homeowner told by Matthew also is named Simon.

The perfume poured out, was it poured on Jesus head or on his feet? Naturally, commentators like to say that it is probably both. What, however, is the intellectual take out from these narratives? After all the personal drama, what can be claimed, both the nameless woman and Mary, came away with, is pure forgiveness! With respect to Mary, forgiveness is reality; although she is assured, her story will be immortalized. The nameless woman's story, along with her, slides into the background and we never hear of her again. It is somewhat sad, because she would have a wild of redemptive story to tell. Her narrative is more intriguing since her life seems to have obvious layers. Stories of forgiveness often tell so much, yet leave much unspoken. There are always two dark sides to a forgiveness story.

The layered story of the nameless woman, without the memorial, has that us-versus-them context. Remember, Jesus listens to those listening in on the conversation Jesus has with the woman who washed his feet. Those other people are snivelling about who can actually forgive sins instead of focus on the fact that sins can be forgiven. "Because you believed, "says Jesus as if to stick it in the face of the snivelers, "you are saved from your sins. Go in peace."[11] Jesus is claiming, when the Believer's sins *are* forgiven, because it means, the Believer is saved from the power of sin. The Believer is authentic and

---

[10] NCV, Matthew 26: 6-13.
[11] NCV, Luke 7: 50.

11

free to begin a new life in the present. However, a few lines previously Jesus tells us, "But the person who is forgiven only a little will love only a little."[12] Perhaps that is why some people today find it difficult to accept forgiveness from Jesus, because they do not believe they are that bad of a person. Forgiveness from God removes the burden of sin and shame and guilt.

---

[12] NCV, Luke 7: 47.

CHRISTIAN SPIRITUALITY

1

Every Christian who believes that the practice of living life with spiritual depth and intellectual authenticity also is aware of their past, pieces of disheveled, screwed up personal history along with the usual normal stuff of life. Most of those "pieces" and "stuff" often seems best left alone. We simply want to leave it in the past where it belongs. Perhaps we cannot really forget the past, unless we have completely forgotten what each of us has said or done. Forgetting is amnesia at its best. Is this kind of amnesia acutely true where there is forgiveness? That is an intriguing question. Such a Christian ought to have the right and privilege not to broadcast their history, regardless how they perceive it even if insignificant, if they do not want to share it. Rather, others should treat that Christian as a new being in Jesus, living their life as God intended.

2

The past no longer has the same hold or attraction. The Christian has a future, not as an extension from the egocentric unredeemed self, but as an extension of the redeemed self, by effect from the death and resurrection of Jesus. It means to become the actual new person who has experienced salvation.

3

Voicing aloud, sometimes, helps to clear up misunderstandings. We're told to get it off the chest. Talk therapy and cognitive rearrangement, they say, helps; which it can. The skeptic might respond, "Voicing it out loud throws it off; avoidance, because destructive words spoken out loud ultimately hang onto the soul as psychological weights." The closure experience therefore often brings philosophical distance between people with a gotcha mentality. Christians should not advocate for the closure process. Closure does not exist! The experiences from our past are a part of who we are. Closure does not remove past experiences. Therefore, salvation seeks to heal by developing the personality, upon the positives and negatives of the identity in personality. We become.

4

Closure is a philosophical fantasy playing word gymnastics to hang the soul, to hang the soul out to dry, exposure to the light of supposed cleansing. However, if there is going to be any experience of closure, it will be between God and the Believer. Whatever psychological closure is and philosophical closure could be evident these are derived from the junkyard of used-up ideas, old humanistic ideological parts that nearly never repair old pieces of the personality. Some old ideas require a lifetime of therapy with no end in sight; pieces of identity are welded together, moving at glacial speed. With God's help, although the person may be slow to catch on, God usually works a bit faster.

5

Christians rather get over their destructive and messy past, by seeing themselves moving on and learn to live with their varied past. This moving on is the healing effect given through the salvation experience with a clean conscience, in spite of themselves.

6

The salvation experience causes the Christian to look at themselves, as God does, that is for who they were and what they now are, and who and what they can become. Salvation cleans up who the Christian was to clear up the way to become the person God has intended. It is the growing process of becoming.

7

Time is life and life is time. That is not clock time. The Believer has the time of their life to grow. Spiritual growth is never fast however. After all, what is hurry? The Believer cannot have more than what they have in the substance of their growth.

8

Writing is a means for discovery, for it seems to draw out from a deep cistern that waters the soul. The discovery is the making of the writer, not only to feel alive, but also to feel for the written process. Authentic insights will flourish. Writing is then a vulnerable revealing of insights. Writing uses words to cut for psychological deep-dive and discover better philosophical understandings. The content of the subject has a context.

9

Definitions are words we use to deal with and describe ourselves. To be more vulnerable as a person who is a Christian means to exercise the reworking of positive words that describes our true relationship with God. We are no longer orphans, without a Parent, Guardian, or with no God and Father who is able to help.

10

As we become older, more seasoned, sadly, regret tears apart the soul; pieces of our definitions and self-worth are torn apart. This can cause us to feel less than we actually are as a person belonging to God and belonging to our own sense of self. We resist being vulnerable, as much as possible, and then we will not feel ripped apart. Confidence in who we are provides courage to resist vulnerability. We learn confidence.

11

When we are open, liable to be more risky and vulnerable, perhaps a bit more fragile, other people would see us for the way we think we actual are as a person. This brings wild thoughts that run amuck: If we were a dirt bag lowlife before becoming a Christian, do others still see us at least slightly mean and mingy? If we were slow on the intellectual draw, do they still see us that way now? If we were uptight and insecure, do others get such vibes from us? If someone had a habit of drinking too much adult beverages, or indulge in a recreational drug, do close friends still watch over us? And, at what point in the Christian's life can such questions no longer be an aspect of their soul and thought pattern? Since God no longer considers such a Christian as out witted by their past, who now is accepted by God, so should that Christian. However, such a Christian, who had less of a secure existence, should not presume their friends, not to be cautious in their acceptance. God would not even attempt such an unwise acceptance of the brand new Christian.

12

Remembering the darkest things about ourselves, that act of recall, can tear apart the soul. Next, regret leaks in like a poison. Regret can distort and obscure positive aspects of personality. Whereas character can be altered through influences from external social conditions. Personality is changed from within; it is altered internally, only by bringing out the positive while the negative lays just below the surface of the personality. The more negativity dies its spiritual death, more freedom is experienced.

Sadly, positive aspects of personality can also be obscured, hidden, remain undeveloped, either by destructive actions by ourselves, and more often than not, due to no fault of our own. Things happen. The power of sin seeks destruction. Therefore, the Christian thanks God for the forgiveness of sins, great and small. That act of being thankful, absolutely removes the poison of regret leaking in from memory. Even the memory of sins, have their destructive power removed.

13

Once we understand what is going on with the kind of person we are and how we became a particular kind of person, then as we Christians, we are obligated to improve upon our personhood and our personality. Such an obligation demands working with the Spirit of God, since it is an integral part of the salvation experience. Otherwise, the imperative for the Christian to be "working to complete your salvation"[13] or "work out your own salvation"[14] would not make much sense. Salvation begins as a gift from God. However, since salvation involves spirituality at its essence, the Christian must think about the implications from salvation. The experience of salvation effects how life is lived and it seeks improvements in personality and character. Who we are and how we become concerns with personal identity. This is soul work.

---

[13] NCV, Philippians 2: 12
[14] ESV, same reference.

14

We can change our character, not our personality. Hidden and unknown aspects of our personality need to be brought to the surface for our attention. What is already present deep within personality, we will attend to them as potential abilities. Often these aspects of personality appear to be more positive than negative. Whereas, character is responsive, acts out, to what is going on around it. Character is made, formed, cut into shape. Salvation is by design meant to heal or save the soul of the real person. The effects of salvation, transcend the deign to only save the soul, rather for the person to have improvements upon character and a wholesome potentials deep in personality are developed, so that the Believer can identify their identity as their own. Deep hidden potentials are brought to the surface of the personality, and as a result, character is shaped and carved, and identified as something better. Salvation deals with who we are, not to change the Believer into what they cannot be. Salvation may be spiritual, but it seeks practical and personal results.

15

Small talk is when we are in conversation about the weather, how the children are, car troubles; the coffee is cheap, blah, blah, and blah. It is not an accidental mistake to refer to small talk as the "ice breaker." Apparently, small talk warms things up what was stone cold. Meanwhile, small talk is nauseatingly polite, patient, waiting for what comes next; it lacks flow and ease, possibly, because it is frozen and slides into nonsense subjects. Small talk can bore anyone to death. Yet, conversation that we have to labor over reveals pieces of ourselves and we may feel vulnerable. Perhaps like gossip, it lubricates and liberates societal relationships; smooth out the rough icy edges to bring depth into our personality. Does God, therefore, consider our prayers small talk and become bored with the whole conversation? God can tolerate small talk because the ice has thawed.

16

There is no spiritual growth without some intellectual development. How else is it possible to know we are growing spiritually? No other way makes it possible to know.

17

Christian beliefs become spiritual when they can transcend the salvation experience as an event. The Christian goes further into what it means to be spiritual and not only labeled as a Christian. By going further into the spirituality of beliefs, the Christian begins to make sense of it all where experience confirms beliefs. There is nothing like experience to confirm an event. Christian spirituality becomes very, very practical. Confirmation by experience firms up, gives the sense, of what is intellectually believed, and is acknowledged as an actuality.

18

Christian Spirituality, can become flighty, soft, without the substance of philosophical understanding accompanied by intelligible critique – like Icarus who would not listen to wisdom but fell flat – will fall flat. The substance of Christian spirituality is reasonable concepts to hold onto which can augment what is believed. Reasonable expansion of knowledge is effective with understanding and reason's power. Therefore, God utilizes the power of reason, with knowledge and understanding, to confirm experience of what is believed. After all, we are convinced to be convicted to be converted. It becomes personal.

19

Beliefs can be philosophically distant – something only to be studied – and is therefore not experienced as an event that does not change the person's life and spiritual condition of being. Ideas and beliefs can become private stuff stuffed into the head. Doubt with cynicism becomes more of a predominant mindset therefore. If there is a salvation experience for such a person, that experience becomes suspect as a psychological head-trip, going nowhere. Christian spirituality is concerned with getting somewhere in personal development, growing to learn to see things as God does. The enemy is not doubt itself of Christian spirituality, however used with cynicism will be used as a tool for obstructionism. Doubt then needs to be doubted. Doubt more often does not clear the way to see, but blocks the view.

If such a Christian wants to throw away their belief in God, disregard spiritual experiences that have effected personal potentials, God often does not get in the way. The learning experience of deep spiritual meaning when accepted as real and effective, without intellectual manipulation, changes how the Christian lives for the rest of their life. Privacy of spirituality within Christianity is an anathema, since secret believing is considered weak, insignificant, out of touch. Persecution for beliefs would be the exception for adherents of Christian spirituality to be secretive; ultimately, distance has not been intellectually embraced, but acknowledged as a possibility.

20

Does anyone, really, need to understand every detail to accept a concept? How would it be known that every detail has been divulged, made evident? For, what matters needs to be able to be practiced. What often is needed and acquired is more information, however, we regularly run with what we understand because it makes sense, particularly when it means an improvement for ourselves.

21

What God wants to accomplish for the Believer's life should not go to waste, ignored. Life then remains as a diminished capacity. The idea is that only the Believer can "destroy the work of God."[15] Spiritual growth that has ceased to grow deeper can dry up and die a lonely death. To grow up spiritually means to grow deeper.

22

In order for Christian spirituality to be an experience, the Christian must transcend the theoretical and go beyond the meaning of the words on the page of the Bible. Christian spirituality develops a maturation for a deeper sense of consciousness and, about God and who the Christian is as a person. Such a spiritual experience permeates personality to bring out better characteristics that are inherent traits or attributes of the personality. Inherent aspects of personality can freely become more prominent. The Christian becomes who they are through the effect and experience of salvation. It means a style of sanctification where feeling clean in the soul conveys the right relationship with God because of accepting Jesus. But, personal faith must be used, exercised. Philosophically it helps to have faith in faith.

23

We do not arrive in this life ready-made, as we would like to be nor as God would like us to be. With help from God, we can become the person we ought to be, the person we cannot help but become. We are imperfect beings. As imperfect beings, we have a spiritual need and a philosophical need, to become more than what we are, to become what God has ultimately intended for us to be. We need a new reputation.

24

The Christian spiritual life involves the idea of sanctification, which is a process after the salvation experience. The effect of sanctification

---

[15] NCV, Romans 14: 20

is completely the work of the Spirit of God. The Believer may read good biblical concepts, learn deeper spiritual insights, but the effect of those concepts and insights upon the personality has a sanctifying purpose to bring out the Believer's improved redeemed self. The Believer understands that as God is working with them in such a method, that process is for their own good. In that method, the Believer is never alone, as if God were oddly separated, off in the distance. God is never against the Believer. Far from it.

25

Christians do not need to drag their lonely past with them. For instance, as an analogy, consider the early North American Indigenous Indian word "travoy" or "travois" (French Canadian, pronounced as "truh-voi"). The travoy is two poles attached on both sides of an animal hide as a platform to transport goods. That travoy was pulled behind a horse. They would load their material belongings on it and drag it as they traveled to various locations. We too can drag behind us our leftover past. Interestingly, from the word "travoy" we get the word "travail" with respect to trouble, hard work, suffering, and like similarities. Likewise, we drag around our psychological past (effect from life) and our philosophical past (how thoughts have useless effects); as we are doing excessive mental anguish, thereby do needless heavy lifting, dragging our history. As a side note, today we have that early Indian concept used as a bicycle trailer, called a travoy. Like its predecessor, it too folds up for easy storage. Fold up the past and relax in God's acceptance and help. Christian spirituality has its gaze forward.

26

Writing to the Corinthians[16] Paul captures the idea that Christians are not alone on their spiritual trek. When Paul penned verse 17, possibly,

---

[16] NCV, chapter 6, verse 17.

he had been influenced by what Jesus had to say: "As you [Father God] are in me [Jesus] and I am in you, I pray that they [Believers] can also be one in us."[17] Irrespective of where Paul's influence is from, amid the context of a flurry of advice to the Corinthian Believers on how to behave and how to think, Paul slips in this nearly unnoticed after thought: "But the one who joins with the Lord is one spirit with the Lord."[18] The sentence is a summation; there are differences between those who live to please God and those who do not have that as their mindset. Apparently, some Christians will be at *one with* God, whereas, some others who profess to be "one spirit with the Lord" but really are not. The point, however, from Paul, the Christian who has the sense of being at one with God, they never should feel alone. This difference of not being alone, but rather connected with God, between some Christians, is an intriguing concept that demands slow assessments about others; not too quick to assume someone may not be connected, just because they appear to be alone. There is a difference between being alone in solitude, than being lonely. The Christian never needs to feel lonely, even in a crowd.

27

We grow spiritually by ourselves, individually, in the presence of God, nobody else can do it for us, no old family reputation or money can buy authentic spirituality with intellectual integrity.

28

Growing spiritually is nothing more than the lifetime sanctification process that explores practical solutions to improve upon personality and character where the self becomes finally free from the power of sin. There is no final arrival as an ultimate perfect condition of being,

---

[17] NCV, John 17: 21.
[18] NCV, 1 Corinthians 6: 17.

however, the sanctified person means to be holy, not sinless although attempting to sin less. An often cited as a descriptive reference what is sanctification, and the reference by Paul informs us in a layered kind of explanation that sanctification is growth: "In the past, some of you were like that,[19] but you were washed clean. You were made holy,[20] and you were made right[21] with God in the name of the Lord Jesus Christ and in the Spirit of our God."[22] Growing spiritual, therefore, evidences for the Christian themselves through practical experiences where their sense of self has improved since they witness for themselves changes in who they are as a person.

29

A fundamental aspect of holiness or living a sanctified life is its settled effect, brings stability, while living out there in the grit of the real world; doing life large, big time – the cloistered life can cramp style, something like bunkered down in the hikers base camp, waiting for the trek up the mountain. The wait and delay may turn emotions inside, however, sometimes we have to wait, as before the Lord, but the desire is to get out and live a holy life. Waiting brings stability. Holiness or sanctification carries with it the residue from stench of the past, except it does not stick. Why? Perhaps, there is no fear when the Christian understands they are holy!

30

Only Matthew records this from Jesus: "So every teacher of the law who has been taught about the kingdom of heaven is like the owner of a house. He brings out new things and old things he has

---

[19] NCV, see verses 9 and 10, in 1 Corinthians 6, lists characteristics of the unrighteous.

[20] ESV, sanctified.

[21] ESV, justified.

[22] NCV, 1 Corinthians 6: 11.

saved."[23] Jesus says this after he was finished teaching the people. In general, the context is the teacher is someone who has spiritual insight, discernment and wisdom, because such a teacher is open to what truth is like as an experience, beyond theoretical speculation. Such a person has treasures deep within their soul, presence, and understand what they know; bring out from their spirituality their philosophical perspectives, building, improving, new ideas from old ideas. Spiritual contents may not change, however spiritual contexts often bring new insights. The soul will otherwise die a slow death for lack of illumination and how to live it in the real world.

31

A positive affirmation that the spiritual life experienced, can therefore be trusted as real, not contrived or invented. We must have a philosophical perspective of what we understand about the knowledge gained regarding our spiritual experiences. To understand what we acknowledge cannot be ignored. Otherwise, all that is obtained is knowledge without experience of spirituality – which invites, is seductively pleasant towards the termination of growing spiritually and intellectually. No affirmation of what is experienced, invites a wedge to split spirituality and intellectuality. Not good.

32

The Christian spiritual journey keeps us moving to deeper understandings. Why, then, do mature and advanced Christians re-read the Bible and extra biblical literature? I suspect there is more to the spiritual journey than learning, although that is a huge stimulating feature. Christian spirituality is a longing that is satisfied, yet, it also has a hunger for more insight, discernment about truth, and the hunt for authenticity. Christian spirituality has a *have-yet* condition of being.

[23] NCV, Matthew 13: 52.

33

The soul is satisfied with understanding, whereas, the intellect wants to know more about what is understood; in this life, that is normal curiosity. However, there is satisfaction in reading the Bible since it seems more personal and less interrupted; it is more quiet and often seems as though we can listen to what we are reading, for that feeds the soul like nothing else can. The *English Standard Version* pins down better the ideas of being quiet and relaxed than some other versions: "Be still before the Lord and wait patiently for him; fret not yourself over the one who prospers over his way, over the man who carries out evil devices."[24] The simple context is for the Believer to wait, be still and rest and relax, which has the connotation of silence. Not always easy, although the experience brings a peace that is satisfaction.

34

The Christian is able to quantify the salvation experience, more than a mere event, but determine and judge, spiritual growth by its subsequent intellectual acknowledgement of what is understood in practical terms: living an authentic life in Jesus as the Savior and out in the real world. Just listening to sermons, does not cut it to grow spiritually – never has and it never will.

35

Wisdom and discernment – these should be two essential characteristics of Christian spirituality. Love is very much at home with these two characteristics; not function properly without love. They may appear separately, but often cannot perform without the other. Wisdom may direct, but discernment has aim. Without wisdom and discernment, Christian spirituality is severely lacking in

---

[24] Psalm 37: 7.

effectiveness and, is diminished and thin. Wisdom and discernment are essential and vital; however, without love working in the background, Christian spirituality's wisdom and discernment have little effect for the direction it seeks and the aim to actually do the job.

36

Wisdom and discernment from the early Christians was not given much attention. What we have however is this admonition from Paul: "We pray that you will also have great wisdom and understanding in spiritual things so that you will live the kind of life that honors and pleases the Lord in every way. You will produce fruit in every good work and grow in knowledge of God."[25] "In him all the treasures of wisdom and knowledge are safely kept."[26] However, elsewhere, the premise is augmented by making it more personal for the Christian who grows spiritually; as such, growth is suggested in the previous citation. The premise pins it, "But solid food is for the mature, for those who have their powers of discernment trained by constant practice to distinguish good from evil."[27] Perhaps, without wisdom and discernment connected with a love reaching down to the core of Christianity, it could have become just another flyby dubious Gnostic cult. Even so, history teaches that Gnosticism came close. It often is that thin line to split the difference that makes the authentic difference.

37

Fortunately, for wise reasons, Christian spirituality has the effect upon the self to be a new self so that the Christian as a person can see what they're all about; after all, that is what God has noticed too,

---

[25] NCV, Colossians 1: 9b, 10.
[26] NCV, Colossians 2: 3.
[27] ESV, Hebrews 5: 14. Compare Matthew 10: 16; Ephesians 1: 17.

what that person is good for. To understand such wise reasons, is for the Christians own wise self-worth as a powerful healing experience.

38

The work of the Spirit of God is to heal an individual's self. That is God's job. This is what it means to be in Christ Jesus, "that you were made free from the power of your sinful self."[28] Paul goes on that all Christians were, "spiritually dead because of your sins and because you were not free from the power of your sinful self, God made you alive with Christ, and he forgave all your sins."[29] The Christian, therefore, is by necessity *not* bound, limited, to their old use-up definition and identity. The Christian has power *not* to drag around their useless past. Perhaps the best method to understand the new self in juxtaposition to the old self, is that the new "me" or new self has been set free from the propensity toward sin, whereas the old self still loves to sin. The Christian has the freedom to make better choices. They can have a new reputation. Face it; this is a thin line between the new and the old. However, as spiritual depth becomes a practice as a condition of being, like wide marker lines on a highway to divide, the demarcations from the new and old are more prominent.

39

To be at peace with God makes it possible to live with God. However, that also provides a relaxed caution. We can be relaxed with God, but we are cautious as to what God will do next, since we do not know everything.

---

[28] NCV, Colossians 2: 11
[29] NCV, Colossians 2: 13

Paul brings home further the concept of what the self is about "May your whole self – spirit, soul, and body – be kept safe and without fault when our Lord Jesus Christ comes. You can trust the One who calls you to do that for you."[30] The Christian can count on God to be careful, full of care, for their "whole self." As Paul reminded the Ephesians, they were "spiritual dead"[31] since humans are "sinful by nature."[32] God, however, through Jesus, "gave us new life."[33] Put it all together, the Christian is free from the power of their egocentric self with its propensity for destruction and for dragging around useless historical memories of long past events. The "sinful nature" refers to the ability, the will, as an innate characteristic to use freedom to commit sin. The use of free will is the freedom of human nature to sin or to do otherwise. To do otherwise is a free act to decide for freedom. It comes natural to sin; to do otherwise is the use of freedom. However, for God it is the other way around: it is natural not to sin. In a few sentences further, Paul assures as we move on, "God made us what we are. In Christ Jesus, God made us to do good works, which God planned in advance for us to live our lives doing."[34] Becoming a sociopath, or a stone cold killer, a parasitic lair, anything similar as those, essentially selfish and destructive, sin sexually, is not what God means to be "made us what we are." Otherwise, the conclusion is that being made in God's likeness (the Genesis narrative) means God's nature is also sinful; it is not. It is a good thing we could not make God after our image, considering how humans can screw things up. That is why salvation offered by God, is freedom from a needy childish insecure self.

---

30 NCV, 1 Thessalonians 5: 23b, 24.
31 NCV, Ephesians 2: 5.
32 NCV, Ephesians 2: 3.
33 NCV, Ephesians 2: 3.
34 NCV, Ephesians 2: 10.

41

Ultimate concerns are about what God wants, which is, who the Believer is as a new person in Jesus and how the Believer is to live life. Frame of reference is shifted from the old egocentric self to the new sense of self because of Jesus.

42

The philosophical proposition: With interest, curiosity, ideas point, towards a future. To be interested in new ideas is a worthwhile position to begin to grow spiritually and to advance intellectually. Regardless of the degree of growth, interest insists there must be a realization more is yet to be grasped. One caveat: if the analysis of ourselves is continuously examined with an old frame of reference, there will be no spiritual growth or intellectual growth. A philosophic diagnostic interest is curious with the search and exploration, to go further into areas of connections and disconnections about personality. Ideas with the future in mind, work with our sense of calling what God wants us to be and do. Therefore, connections and disconnections are about hidden talents and traits that appear to be stifled, unrealized and unknown. God wants each Believer to discover their potentials; not feel suppressed, forced out-of-sight, stiff and one-dimensional, lacking a future.

43

Christian spirituality is very much at home with a theistic existential condition of being, because both are concerned about authenticity and how that is consciously experienced. Otherwise, it would be antithetical to the style of Christian spirituality that acknowledges a philosophic diagnostic interest. Experience brings the familiar of being at home, which is a place of trust.

44

Is there a shadow side to Christian spirituality? Probably the most disturbing dark shadow side of the spirituality of Christianity is the inability to comprehend human nature and God's nature. An incorrect understanding of those two natures, constructs the divisions in theology between classic Arminianism and Calvinism. The shadow side often is inordinately consumed with its own self, a narcissistic giddy enthusiasm that believes, it is within the nature of God to have chosen each Believer individually. Rather, God chooses everyone to believe and those that believe in God obviously are chosen corporately as an entitled or labelled group of Christians, because they chose to believe. Paul tells Timothy, "that those whom God has chosen," ultimately I'd add, "can have the salvation that is in Christ Jesus."[35] As it says here, "can have" or "may obtain"[36] clearly refers to a free choice that each must decide, even though the context is corporate and not individual. God chose all to believe in him, but humans have the will to reject him, to do otherwise. Nowhere in Scripture does it claim that an individual is chosen for salvation; that would be a forced interpretation of Scripture. The Timothy reference may be basis for the shadow side of the spirituality of Christianity, however instigated only by some Christians.

45

Jesus is speaking to a woman fetching water at a public well. With irony, Jesus says for anyone to hear, "Everyone who drinks this water will be thirsty again, but whoever drinks the water I give will never be thirsty. The water I give will become a spring of water gushing up from that person, giving eternal life."[37] When a Christian becomes

---

[35] NCV, 2 Timothy 2: 10.
[36] This is the ESV rendering.
[37] NCV, John 4: 13, (context, verses 5-15).

interested in the deeper insightful side of their spirituality, there is a learning experience. This experience is like a spring of water that flows with ease from the soul, from their internal reality. Jesus is telling us the soul can become satisfied. Soul work may be interested in deeper understandings; however, the satisfaction[38] derives from within, not from external sources.

46

The soul's interest is a desire and a hunger, better yet, a longing that isn't entirely taken away, rather the longing is properly directed; a sense of nourishment has been achieved, although there is more to come. The cruel and reckless cravings have lost their stimulus. What is experienced is a peace that is satisfaction. The water from the soul still gushes, but running around trying to discover what satisfies, loses interest.

47

In John chapter four, the story that Jesus claims the individual "will be thirsty" first infers there is a spiritual longing. Jesus presumes longing is understood. If an individual has no interest or curiosity to pay attention to their longings, with respect to what longings reveal, is lethargy. Lethargy is close to spiritual anaesthesia, not caring for activity, ought not to be confused as spiritual death, although it could. The satisfaction – "never be thirsty"– Jesus offers assures spiritual longings will flow but now with "eternal life."[39] The spring has not gone dry.

---

[38] Compare Proverbs 19: 23.
[39] NCV, verses 13, 14.

GET PERSONAL

1

For new Initiates to Christian spirituality, faith, above all else, makes sense of the spiritual life or way of being spiritually minded. Overall, faith is thrown into a new methodology of thinking and living, which will prove to be difficult intellectually, to sort out details between faith and reasoned concepts. Some take a leap of faith and accepted God and what God has to offer, and went for it. No fancy pants theological sophist arguments were going to convince any further; such is a reasonable expectation due to faith. Whereas, others needed the arguments, the back and forth logic to make more sense of what faith is like, and what God is like. Between those two approaches, the soul's needs reach where faith can be exercised. Come hell or high water that had to be settled and reasonably accepted. It is what the soul desires, what convinces.

2

Believing in God has to be real and practical for the soul to be satisfied. Part of that believing and satisfaction means that, "Without faith no one can please God. Anyone who comes to God must believe that he is real and that he rewards those who truly want to find him."[40]

---

[40] NCV, Hebrews 11: 6. Compare James 4: 8, "Come near to God and God will come near to you."

Therefore, belief in God, to be satisfying it first must acknowledge the existence of God, otherwise, belief is vacuous and only a concept neatly tucked into the head. Does any thinking person, on their own, take the initiative to find God? Of course. Anyone can. Frequently the unthinking person may necessitate a convincing nudge, in the first place, from the Spirit of God to believe in God. What Jesus says, however, "No one can come to me unless the Father draws,"[41] – we today would roughly pin it as, compels, persuades, to exert influence as though freely and willingly to comply, just enough to be convinced to believe. This is the sense of what it means to be drawn along by God. God puts enough pressure on to persuade, leading, without any necessary predetermined outcome, because of the free will aspect of the freedom of human nature.

To be persuaded by God means, to be convinced to be convicted to be converted. It is similar to the word "advertise," which indicates to *advert, to turn* –literally our heads and emotions. As in advertising so in spiritual persuasion, the attempt to be convinced (confidently conquer doubt, reasonably satisfied, overcome objections) to be convicted (acknowledged already to be convicted of a need) to be converted (to revert from a perversion, to converge to what is better, to turn to something else from another). Through this process of God draws us out, persuades us to "come" to Jesus, although the culmination outcome, to freely decide by the potential Believer. The Believer is persuaded to turn away and turn towards belief, not turned to be forced towards belief. Conversion must have sense of its meaning to be convincing for a conviction.

3

It was hell the first two years of my Christian life. I had faith enough. I also had an expectation and curiosity about my faith that God began to change my life. Beyond that, I did not know what was coming. I

---

[41] NCV, John 6: 44a.

was unsettled, dissatisfied, and speculation was drenched in doubt: Where is this supposed peace with God and myself? First, I had belief in God, then no belief in God. Suddenly, another decision had to be made. The conclusion was that the unsettled emotions were not about faith nor whether to stop believing in God. What I was dealing with was the psychological differences and the philosophical differences that involved a shift of consciousness and a way of being. I simply relaxed, stepped back, and began thinking of myself, as God knows all about my potentials. That was it. That philosophical realization brought stability. God understands and appreciates each of us for the kind of person we can be.

4

When I became a Christian, thoughts about truth, my interests, the soul — these things came alive intellectually — with a distinct philosophical instinct or discernment that spirituality from God does not cause a person to be unintelligent. If there is a form of cultural Christian spirituality that causes us to feel stupid and simple — then dump it. Authentic Christian spirituality will never cause anyone to feel unintelligent.

5

The insight or illumination associated with my new and different spiritual mindset is like coming alive as if for the first time. I loved it. However, more questions popped up after believing in God than before. When alive spiritually, more questions arouse intellectual curiosity. Answers feed the soul with spiritual nourishment.

6

When there is an archetypal shift in frame of reference, as coming alive spiritually and intellectually, perchance, memory can stir pinching scenes from the past. There were some uninformed adults in my life. I distinctly recall being told as a child, "Don't ask so many questions." Children are seen, not heard. Now as a new Christian, I discovered I had freedom to ask questions, and there were answers. Questions about how to think and what to think; how to live a spiritual life, dig deep into meaning and nourish the soul, faith, and confidence to be a courageous person. To avoid poking around with questions is the cause for weakness.

7

Some people may wince a bit at what is next. As maturity advanced, I discovered an integrity of being at home in a philosophical temperament. I noticed it before, but did not know such is my nature. This leads to particular points of view. As a thinking Believer and as a person, each of us should come to terms where we fit in, belong. There are conservative, liberal, progressive, Christian labels or nametags. Further along with other sub-groups, including Catholicism. Two main groups are the Arminian (Jacobus Arminius) theological perspective and the other has a Calvinistic (John Calvin) theology. With the exclusion of Catholicism, lurking behind all other Christian groups is those two are predominant theological perspectives. It is very wise to know that, for it alters how the Bible is read and taught. Theologically, I did not care about Arminianism or Calvinism, as they bored. I had a poor philosophical position about theology. Many Christians either ignore the difference or put up with it. From my early Christian life, I had a natural, innate aversion toward Calvinism. Catholicism was and still is, utterly unconvincing; represents form over substance; in spite of my reading of Karl Rahner. Years later, my intellectual lean toward Arminian theology was fixed. I found then and still discover Arminian theology less forced with regard to interpretation of the Bible. This causes it to be intellectually honest, intelligible.

The intention here is not to get too far in the tall grass on the subject of the differences between Arminianism and Calvinism, which is not that much, but namely a philosophical difference on how to think intelligibly. The Arminian and Calvinist divide has been my critical aspect that informed my philosophical theology. As much as we admire John Calvin's intellectual tenacity, he seems to be too anxious and insecure, when he did not have to be. An excessive interest in the letter of the word instead of the spirit of the word permitted gruesome fires that gave Calvin a license to kill anyone whom he thought a heretic. Nowadays, if old Calvin would be around, most people would tell him to grow up and get a grip. You know – maybe drink more beer instead of lighting people on fire. A dark question: Has Calvin's insecurity leaked through his theology? One sure impression, Calvinists like everything to be ordered, determined, without mishap or perchance, regardless of the banality of evil or the extravagance of good or the freedom of human nature. Something appears neurotic. They have a fetish drive to describe the sovereignty of God in monotone singularity that reminds more of a philosophy than a theology.

A short list of books for your investigation. These are in alphabet order by author. *The Soul of Doubt* (2016), Dominic Erdozain; *For Calvinism* (2011), Michael Horton; *The New Chosen People* (1999), William Klein; *Against Calvinism* (2011), Roger Olson; *Arminius Speaks* (2011), ed., John Wagner. Since I have read these books, they are recommended in good conscience. Accordingly, there is plenty of freedom to accept Jesus as Savior or to reject Jesus, regardless of any theological perspective.

8

God works with what he has to work with. God works with our personality, not against who we are.

9

All of us bring to the experience of salvation everything that we are as a person – "Just as I am, without one plea" – as the bittersweet song encourages to repent without fabricated excuses; itself is not an exaggeration. Charlotte Elliott (1788-1871)[42] first penned those words in a poem. Her words poured out from an angry crushed disposition, making it a confessional for future broken people to accept their existential condition, to allow God to build upon it a future. God does that construction and reconstruction work.

10

Told to believe in God gets a bit old because thinking ceases therefore. Faith then pants longingly and just hangs there. Authenticity and faith expect more than the sophist's rambling.

11

Authenticity carries with it authority with a convincing weight. Authenticity is added to that which matters. Is God without authenticity? It is inconceivable to consider God as not being authentic by being himself, by who God is. Otherwise, God would be incomplete. Theology does not list authenticity as an attribute belonging God. Yet, can we conceive of any of God's attributes without authenticity?

12

Skeptic's claim that spirituality is a psychological head-trip. "It's only in the head," skeptics doubtfully insist, "Like a contrived fantasy, psychologized theological ideas presented neatly in philosophical phraseology, but wrapped in biblical words." Then, the Believer would have to deny their senses that are due to the changes produced, simply as an act of faith and the effect from the Spirit of God. It does not appear unreal, contrived, or imagined. Not just salvation is

---

[42] Wikipedia.org.

experienced as a real event. There is an experience of an experience, which cannot be contrived.

13

Spirituality and rationalism are frequently closely associated therefore. Rationalism is the handmaiden to authentic Christian spirituality but not identified as spiritual.

14

If what we know and understand is only mental gymnastics, without further improvement on how life is to be lived as God intended, then we are a boring pedantic and possibly ineffective as a person and as a Christian. Therefore, when there is a breach between the distinctions of the rational and the practical, Christian spirituality will balk at the imbalance. Where life is loaded down with imbalance, life becomes restless, ineffective, and dissatisfied. Often such a person, no matter how spiritually enlightened, becomes irritable, impatient, without any longings satisfied.

15

The words from Jesus make sense and carry long-term meaning: "Come to me, all of you who are tired and have heavy loads, and I will give rest. Accept my teachings and learn from me, because I am gentle and humble in spirit, and you will find rest for your lives. The burden that I ask you to accept is easy; the load I give you to carry is light."[43] Anyone who wants to believe, to accept Jesus teachings and learn, will discover relief from the imbalances of life, the continuous tiresome search for satisfaction and longing for peace. Such a search will "find" because Jesus will "give" which is able to transform what

---

[43] NCV, Matthew 11: 28-30.

we carry around into an easy weight that is manageable, can be dealt with, because we can "learn" to relax and "accept" what Jesus has said. There is no heavy lifting to make sure the correct ideology has been thought through, just right. As if, the soul could not be satisfied. Jesus gives an easy peace of acceptance by learning.

16

The Christian's whole life is redeemed, given back, as it should be. Redemption is given by God's acceptance as the person was, as they are, and as they shall become. Further, this is the process of sanctification, becoming better than before, through spiritual growth as it is learned how to think and live a life that pleases God and is satisfying for the Believer. In that practice, faith is not blind faith, but it has results noticed in spiritual maturation.

7

From the entire Psalm 32, it expresses the contemporary Christian spiritual content about psychological freedom from the past. Psalm 32 deals with the freedom from sins of the past and freedom from being needy or afflicted for constant reassurance. Christian spirituality has the wisdom not to tolerate for long a cheap constant need for reassurance.

18

Freedom as cited in the New Testament is be *the* classic definition with respect to salvation as a freedom. This time, salvation is a lived experience goes outside the head, takes the heady ideas of salvation out into the real world. Paul writes, "We have freedom now, because Christ made us free. So stand strong. Do not change and go back into slavery of the law."[44] Strength to stand freely means there is an

---

[44] NCV, Galatians 5: 1.

opposing force. The Believer is free from family psychological history and the power of sin. There is no need to "go back" to an unhealthy negative family history that can enslave. The old adage that blood runs thicker than water needs to be kicked to the curb. Sure, there will always be a family – heritage, pedigree, ancestry, old stock – a connected family, to culture and sociological traditions linked to ourselves. Except now, they have less connection for their grip has no power. With help from God, the past can be reconstituted so that the effect from the past, however important or good it may have been, is changed. Not everything from the past is entirely negative. What is considered positive can hold back our maturation. Therefore, the entirety of our past is redeemed. Primitive hangers-on from ancestry's past with its old stock and trade in family name, becomes a fixation with no end in sight. Our past creeps upon us with an uneasy roar through memory. Dead things from the past are real killers.

19

Human nature is freedom. As a freedom, human nature is not entirely good nor bad, but has the propensity to be willful towards what is good and bad, however, often for evil intentions. That is the power of sin. Freedom is the nature of God, therefore, the human's nature is freedom because we are made after the likeness of God. The theistic existentialist philosopher, Peter Koestenbaum posits in *the New Image of the Person*, "To the extent that I am a *freedom* I feel hope, energy, and control. But as a freedom, I am also outside of the material and objective realm of things; in relation to the world my freedom is a supreme mystery and a sublime miracle."[45] Arguably, where there is no opposition we will not fully realize how free we actually are; this takes the experience of freedom beyond theory and out into practical life. Accordingly, Koestenbaum explains, "Furthermore, the structure of consciousness tells us that a person is

---

[45] P.129.

41

by nature free. Intelligence and freedom go together, for freedom is lucidity about actions and directions."[46] When we are conscious, well aware of our surroundings and ourselves and what we do we know we are free. Koestenbaum again, "Strictly speaking, inauthenticity and neuroticism are therefore not the destruction of freedom but the use of freedom to repress the use of freedom *and* the use of freedom to repress the knowledge of this repression."[47] Such a statement could very well be an apt description of how the power sin can limit freedom as an attempt to repress freedom as an authentic style of the condition of being and of spirituality.

Repression therefore, explains the spiritual slackness and/or spiritual destruction of the soul. Repression requires insight, the light of truth to see freedom for the life it embodies. This light of truth and the life of freedom is given by Jesus is to reach through the repression of what stairs back from the spiritual slackness. As John executes it effectively, "In him there was life, and that life was the light of all people. The Light shines in darkness, and the darkness has not overpowered it."[48] "Through risk we become aware that the anxiety of freedom can be tolerated," affirms Koestenbaum, "that freedom is our nature, and that it *feels good* to integrate into our total personality."[49] Freedom brings its own responsibility and we accept it for then we feel alive, and we are aware that anxiety comes with responsibility. Some people are frozen with fear, freeze-dried into pieces falling apart, fearful, full of fear, because freedom gives options, choices, and they sooner would live with ignorance as a bliss; therefore less anxiety. Ignorance is bliss is to be unfree (allusion to Socrates).

Koestenbaum has told us, freedom is applied to be free, from our destructive and neurotic self. It explains what it is like to be free in

---

[46] P.160.

[47] P.301.

[48] NCV, John 1: 4, 5. Compare 1 John 1: 7, the Christian lives in "light" as God does. Moreover, the short three letters is usually attributed to John who wrote the fourth gospel, although the author is not identified, than by the "elder."

[49] P.328.

a relationship with God with our new sense of self. The experience of freedom within human nature, and the freedom as augmented by God, is because of salvation and redemption through Jesus. The Christian then can use their freedom of their nature to live the life of faith with an enhanced, undetermined freedom. The person who has their nature redeemed knows experientially: it means to see themselves as more than just a person, but as people to be a freedom.

20

A redeemed human nature is freer to be free from the effects of the power of sin. Jesus says it himself, "If you continue to obey my teaching, you are truly my followers. Then you will know the truth, and the truth will make you free."[50] However, there is a counter argument from Jesus' whinny objectors (v.33) that they were never "slaves." The comeback from Jesus is, "who lives in sin is a slave to sin,"[51] finishing off the verbal banter with, "So if the Son makes you free, you will be truly free." [52]Jesus has the authority to speak as the Son of God.[53] The impression from John, the whole chapter eight, the intellectual banter between Jesus and his objectors, that Jesus presents himself as the inside man who knows it all stance, and the objectors are on the outside looking in, somewhat speechless. Classic rhetoric.

21

Experience in relationship with God must have a knowledge that is participatory and thus personal. The relationship involves God who is knowable. Does God have the need to be known? God, likes to be known by people. Does that necessarily indicate need?

---

[50] NCV, John 8: 31b, 32
[51] NCV, v.34.
[52] NCV, v.36.
[53] See Matthew 3: 17; 17: 5.

22

John records Jesus who makes the claim that God is knowable. Quoting Jesus, who is praying for his Followers, "And this is eternal life: that people know you, the only true God, and that they know Jesus Christ, the One you sent."[54] The word "know" is to obtain experiential personal knowledge, which differentiates from mere knowing about God as a theoretical concept. Marvin Vincent informs that the Greek *ginosko* for "know" means, "eternal life consists in knowledge, or rather the *pursuit* of knowledge, since the present tense marks *a continuance, a progressive* perception of God in Christ. That they might *learn to know*."[55] Such knowledge is not skimming over the surface, like a quick perusal of knowing, just enough, of God. The sense is that the Believer can learn to know more and more with respect to who and how God is like in a personal manner; such learning is long term, as far as the relationship can deepen. A relationship with God has freedom to loosen things up so learning is personally experienced, as an advanced depth with wisdom and discernment and love.

23

Again, Paul gets it right: "You were taught to leave your old self – to stop living the evil way you lived before. That old self becomes worse, because people are fooled by the evil things they want to do. But you were taught to be new in your hearts, to become a new person. That new person is made to be like God – made to be truly good and holy."[56] There may be a learning curve since they are to be "taught" and simply "stop" living, as though, they did not have a new self. Just simply stop it, stop doing what ultimately works against them. In

---

[54] NCV, John 3: 17.
[55] *Word Studies in the New* Testament, vol.2, p.263.
[56] NCV, Ephesians 4: 22-24.

BECOMING AS GOD INTENDED

addition, apparently, "be like God" is not that difficult, when it is considered being "truly good and holy."

Compare a further exploration what Paul nails down to the Ephesians. Paul lays it out that, "You can follow sin, which brings spiritual death, or you can obey God, which makes you right with him."[57] "Take your pick; make up your mind. Be free or not. Know that you will die a slow spiritual death," Paul seems to say. He goes on, "because this is hard for you to understand,"[58] that it is a matter of making an intelligent decision not to be a "slave to sin."[59] Rather because of salvation, Paul reminds Believers that they can choose to live as actually they "were made free from sin, and now you are slaves to goodness."[60] The whole concept pins down to either stop doing what ought not to be done and by necessity, avoid spiritual death, and become alive like God, as God cannot help but be. Unless persecution is unavoidable, it is a choice.

24

Freedom in Christian spirituality, while associated with free will, which is also freedom of human nature, signifies not to be locked into the past nor by the power of sin. To be, nonetheless, unfree screams out from a human being disconnected from the freedom of Christian spirituality, to be less human, since they are less free. Perhaps, such an unfree human being functions from a limited expression and, only by instincts and biology; mode of being is one-dimensional animalistic. To be unfree is first to be philosophically primitive, because the thinking is simple, narrow, and uncomplicated; next, as a condition of being such a human is a psychological cripple or constricted with limited expression for positive emotions. The outcome is for such a human being is their internal reality or soul is anesthetized, numbed,

---

[57] NCV, Romans 6: 16.

[58] V.19.

[59] NCV, Romans 6: 17.

[60] NCV, v.19. The ESV has "slaves to righteousness."

towards that which matters. Biology, therefore, is not destiny, but a free spiritual awakening, is destiny.

25

God never changes personality! Indeed, never will God violate the essence of personality. God will work with the personality we have, bring out and evolve, better and positive aspects, but God does not alter the essentials of personality. God will change character and identity; however, never ever will God change the personality. Indeed, God changes the way we think and consequently how we live by improving on better aspects of the self. Therefore, to be born again is *to be a new self*. After all the spiritual growing (pains) and intellectual advancements, deep within the soul of such a person's personality, there is a constant familiarity to be connected with identity and character; otherwise there could be paranoia.

26

Probably the philosopher's *aha experience* occurs when sudden insight flashes through consciousness, because a concept is often suddenly grasped, before it disappears. The concept, idea, and outline, precedes the insight. Note to self: always make notations. Concepts are conceived conceptions.

27

Salvation and growing spiritually combined, is not an egocentric psychological fantasy head-trip; it may appear that way at times because it brings alive the sense of self, but as a new redeemed self. If anything, the experience of salvation and growing spiritually is a philosophical head-trip, because there is a complete archetype shift on how to deal with the self. Paul says it nicely, "Yes, when Christ died, he dies to defeat the power of sin one time – enough for all time. He now has a new life, and his new life is with God. In the same way, you should see yourselves as being dead to the power of sin and alive with God through Jesus Christ."[61] The Christian must make the conscious decision to see themselves in a new frame of reference. This means not to be philosophically swayed to the negative and neurotic influences of the old self, but be alive to the positive and philosophically advantageous influences of the new self, which is an improved personality and character. More than that however, the outlook for the Christian is to be anew in God as Jesus is in new in God. There is an interesting theology here. Jesus is new in God because of what he went through for our redemption; for Jesus it is finished, a done deal. The Christian is new in God for what they are becoming; for them it is beginning, with more growth.

28

It is not the pseudo-Christian Paul writes to, rather the authentic Christian. He puts it pointedly: "As you received Christ Jesus the Lord, so continue to live in him. Keep your roots deep in him and have your lives built on him. Be strong in the faith, just as you were taught, and always be thankful."[62] Those verses ooze with authenticity for the authentic Christian: there is actuality with confidence. However, further on Paul reminds Christians: "When you were spiritually dead because of your sins and because you were not free from the power of your sinful self, God made you alive with Christ, and he forgave all our sins."[63] A spiritual death, has death dripping from its own deathly meanings, and has the effect to suck the life out of life, the stuff life is made of which is spirit and destiny; it turns back on itself since there is a power struggle within the nature of sin, narcissistically produced by a wilful pride. Nothing good comes from that. The individual who

---

[61] NCV, Romans 6: 10, 11.
[62] NCV, Colossians 2: 6, 7.
[63] NCV, v.13.

chooses to become alive spiritually, thereby often discovers their own person, as God has intended for them to be, likewise discovers, after the fact, how dead they were in comparison to what it is like being alive spiritually.

Born to Become

1

Each of us is born with certain abilities. An ability is what we can do, while a capability is the proficiency, the knowhow on working with our abilities. Aptitudes are unique abilities that come naturally. However, there are tasks some of us can accomplish with the greatest of ease and even improve on what could be done. Experience on the job has that effect. Experience brings familiarity that is trusted. While another person struggles because the task is not natural, or abilities are poorly developed as skills. They have entered unfamiliar territory. God utilizes our abilities, regardless, for his purposes, to help others and, so we can have a better and more effective life as it is lived, deeply experienced. When, however, we are not free or do not feel free, to express our abilities, might be for various reasons. Reasons that impede or block our expression of an ability, might either be a personality disorder that has been pushed into the foreground, or a lack of character, an addiction, and a lack of training and experience. More often, many people simply feel forgotten and ignored, and fall through the cracks of the societal system. Comparisons between themselves and other talented people conclude they have limitations. Disappointment and insignificance must be wrestled off therefore. Comparisons with others can be positive and negative, encouraging and destructive. Comparison, nonetheless, with the ubiquitous self-absorbed squeaky-clean individual who has more pride than guilt – these must be ignored. God certainly will deal with any convoluted mess of comparisons we can make with others. God loves to fix people, for their own good, of course. The practical result is people have to learn to work with their abilities and the limitations. Let God sort out the details of messy comparison that should not take up our time.

2

God redeems the whole personality, what that person inherently has and who they potentially will become, as a particular personality. Personality has inherent potential abilities, which is learnt how to be expressed. The work of the Spirit of God is to cause each of us to discover and explore hidden and unknown potentialities deep within our personality. This is how God uses or works with people to be an encouragement to others and for themselves. Whatever is inherent within our personality, God will utilize our abilities through the expression of our personality because it is a match; it fits with who we are as a person. If we want to accomplish something but cannot express it effectively through our personality, then perhaps we do not have that ability. God will not force an unnatural inept ability to be used as a gift or skill. What we have has to fit with reality.

3

God does take who we are, with flawed character and eccentric personality, and God actually believes he can do something with us. God will help us to develop a particular skill, suited for us, which will invariably be a source of encouragement for others. Otherwise, there is incongruity between who we think we are and our connection with reality.

4

If God can believe and think great ideas about us, what prevents us from thinking big too? We just need to know our reasonable limitations.

5

Probably the most effective style of Christian spirituality can assist other people is to be an exemplar, without any direct contact. Encouragement is caught, not taught. The exemplar is an example that emanates from their very being, from their own personality and presence. This is not such a farfetched idea.

6

Paul, as a teacher, an exemplar, and apostle, expressed the concept that every Believer has responsibility to be an exemplar as a means of encouragement to others. Paul in an instructive mode politely tells us, "Brother and sisters, all of you should try to follow my example and copy those who live the way we showed you."[64] Could any of us have such confidence, moxie, and authority to tell more than one person to follow our example? Do we have what it takes, for our sense of self, to view and present ourselves as an exemplar?

7

Paul puts himself up as an exemplar for the early Christians and for us. All the same, Paul admits he did not have it all together, put in a neat philosophical and psychological package, standing out from a weak identity. There also is an open, yet, a slightly cautioned bravado. Paul explains, "I do not mean that I am already as God wants me to be, I have not yet reached that goal, but I continue trying to reach it and to make it mine."[65] He says positively that since he is "trying" he is going to become as God intended, because Paul knows it is "mine" to obtain.

---

[64] NCV, Philippians 3: 17.
[65] NCV, Philippians 3: 12.

8

From Paul, we get a glimpse into a deeper longing and yearning, that nearly goes unnoticed: "Now I know only a part, but then I will know fully, as God has known me."[66] From that verse 12b, it does not refer to the infamous "painful physical problem" mentioned in 2 Corinthians 12: 7; also described as a "thorn was given in the flesh" (ESV). What we have in verse 12b, Paul has a longing to understand himself, as God understands Paul. Paul wanted to know what God knew about Paul, and Paul wanted to know what that knowledge was for himself. That is normal curiosity. This longing to know, remained with Paul all his shortened lifetime, and helped to fulfill his calling.

From verse 12 quoted, Paul informs us there will arrive a future time (heaven?), "we shall see clearly." Paul, however, pushes the longing idea as he turns from the plural "we" to the singular "I." To repeat, "Now I know only a part, but then I will know fully, *as God has known me*" (emphasis added). Paul has just expressed a philosophical concept about a spiritual or psychological longing. He wants to know, apparently, what he did not know, or he suspected there is more to his personality than he may have known. That is drive! How many people attempt to understand themselves?

Intriguingly, God gave Paul profound spiritual insight for the very purpose to bring reason and intellectual content to Christian spirituality. Which Christianity needed. Yet, by the ability Paul had, God used. In spite of abilities, they caused Paul to contend or cope with (potential) conceit as he claims for himself, "I would become too proud of the wonderful things shown me, a painful physical problem was given me. This problem was a messenger from Satan, sent to beat me and keep me from being too proud."[67] So, when

---

[66] NCV, 1 Corinthians 13: 12b.

[67] NCV, 2 Corinthians 12: 7. The ESV has "harass" instead of "beat," and the Authorized Version has "buffet." Appears Paul was given a rap, a tap or nudge, enough to irritate. Either way, it prevented Paul from the potential to be "too" conceited. See verse 9b which lends to the idea it's only a potential.

Paul talks about being an exemplar in Philippians, there is a lot of experiential credibility and personal authoritative weight behind what he instructs. As Paul puts it, behind Paul's longings, is the desire is to be "as God wants me to be," confidently saying, "I continue trying to reach it and to make it mine."[68] Today we call it street cred.

Still, with his spiritual longings and intellectual hunger (these complement each other) he took his weaknesses and reconstituted them as strengths. Those abilities are a driving force that caused him to stand tall. Paul speaks with confidence, all the same, "So I am very happy to brag about my weaknesses. Then Christ's power can live in me."[69] Paul still has some swagger, for he reveals that sentence just after saying he might have a problem of being "too proud" because of what he knows. A wise nugget here: Because something is from God, does not suggest there will not be any inherent problems we must contend with.

9

James Hillman has this to say about authority: "There is a kind of power given neither by control, by office, not by prestige, and can't be achieved by ambition. Reputation is some of it, but only some. This is the power of authority."[70] Authority carries the person. Hillman goes on, to know when we encounter someone with authority, by extension, and they are an exemplar and have authenticity packed into personality. "Was it how they carried themselves," Hillman queries, "or reacted at a critical moment? Was it their aura of distance or their easiness, so at home in the world? One thing seems sure: they made you feel the power of authenticity. They simply had it within themselves."[71]

Hillman wants to know more about authority. He correctly

---

[68] NCV, Philippians 3: 12
[69] NCV, 2 Corinthians 12: 9
[70] *Kinds Of Power*, p.160.
[71] Ibid, p.165.

insists, "Authority is more than knowledge, memory, judgment, competence, social relations; more than who you know and where you've been. . . . it is an invisible quality, it also attracts great envy and its authenticity is demeaned . . . [it is] what the Romans called *gravitas*, a certain weight that gives importance, even an oppressive seriousness."[72] Gravitas causes the person who has the authenticity of authority to acquire the weight or power to convince with serious intentions. Hillman again, "Perhaps, authority rises as the soul sinks gravely – graveward – as one becomes an ancestor, a figure who represents the stored wisdom of the community, a representation rather than a personality."[73] Authority arrives as the soul becomes wise. Authority carries and presents the person who has it as a packaged identity with character.

However, Hillman has not lost sight that the power of authority must be persuasive therefore. "Listening to empty rhetoric," he sounds off, "we have the feeling we've heard it all before, and many times. The real thing lifts you to your feet and turns your head, the course of your life permanently swayed toward a new direction – just by the power of words."[74] Authority has the weight and convincing power of words particularly as an expression of what our personality and character, has to offer.

Paul hardly said anything about authority. Except, his advice to Titus, where Paul uses the word "authority."[75] Titus is told to, "encourage the people and tell them what is wrong in their lives, with all authority. Do not let anyone treat you as if you were unimportant."[76] Authority has confidence to speak up when it is called for. Never forget that.

---

[72] Ibid, p.165.

[73] Ibid, p.165.

[74] Ibid, p.171.

[75] *Kinds Of Power.*

[76] NCV, Titus 2: 15.

10

The authentic Christian does not need to be timid as to fear their own sense of authority to authorize a worthwhile life; also pleases God. Otherwise, they may entomb their own possible definition of their own new self from salvation. Timidity kills growth.

11

There is much hope laid out when a mere individual becomes an authentic person, rooted deep in their Christian spiritual experience; confidence and authority to speak and live, since there's an "oppressive seriousness"[77] (Hillman) so that the spiritual experience becomes more alive, focused and attention driven. They have a new reputation with a distinct power and authority that comes from God.

12

The soul is the internal reality of who we are. The soul is presence of that internal reality. Self-awareness reveals the internal reality, which is the soul revealing its presence. It is the soul, not a split or duel personality, because there is no estrangement but a constant familiarity causes connections with one's own self and with other people.

13

Satisfaction and some tension will acknowledge a contently discontented condition of being. Recognition that personality eccentricities we are born with, will never cause the personality to be what it cannot become. That is because there is a constant familiarity deep within the self of the personality. Such a person is not estranged

---

[77] *Kinds Of Power*, p.165.

from their own self, therefore will not feel alone for who they are. Personality is often content with itself whereas its eccentricities flare up odd discontentment from time to time. It could be a good balance, which evidences a person's abilities and, their identity and character

14

Feelings are not thoughts. Identity is not how to feel about our own sense of self and our own soul or internal reality. There can be an emotion about an idea, and then express it with a definite feeling for it. Otherwise, there is sociopathy at worst, disordered and disrupted, disturbed and used-up at best, leading to confusion and be hyperactive sensitive about identity. Nothing positive comes from that feeling.

15

To know without a doubt, that God is working with the personality should authorize with personal authority to make it possible for the Christian to demonstrate, show off, they can be at home with who they are; they trust the process of God's work since they are connected, not estranged, with their personality. However, this authority and being at home is not a license to sin, destroy, or act as one pleases. The Christian utilized by God as an exemplar, is not for inappropriate gains for the Christian. The Christian is confident within their own self to be an exemplar. Therefore, personality is not disconnected from identity and character. Otherwise, personal existence runs amuck, with no consciousness about special effects produced by God's work with the personality. Each of us have our own idiosyncratic personality, for sure, but God is working with us, not against us, to cause our uniqueness to be an advantage for us and for the sake of others; it cannot be any other way.

16

Christians, who have been the recipient of patience and love from other Christians, have a greater consciousness of special effects resulting from patience and love. I have, nonetheless, seen some Christians who have been recipients of such patience and love, yet, they were unable to receive it fully, if at all, since there has been too much psychological hurt, too much philosophical suspicion, deep in their internal reality. Sometimes healing takes time, even though the special effects of salvation, such as sanctification or maturation, have worthwhile results. Each personality has its own unique soul that acts and reacts; it seems, on its own timetable. No human being is born to stagnate, resist love, and claim to be normal. We become who we should be, often just as we cannot but be otherwise – just in time to receive patience and love and to give it away. We become, all in good time, as they say. However, hanging on too long to hurts and suspicions, works against the time of our life.

17

Jesus meets a woman at a well.[78] He insists and convinces her, he has a type or style of water that springs from the soul, which is authentic spirituality and it gives eternal life, to the person who believes. Jesus offers a spiritual style of water, however, that does not mean it will flow with ease all the time. The flow of spiritual style of aliveness is always present, but intellectual concerns, psychic hurts, and weird suspicions, can cause that flow to a trickle. What happens next, some Believers lose heart and courage, feelings of falling through the cracks of society to be forgotten. Out of sight and out of mind – in both sense of the word. Such people are crestfallen; their soul sinks, and frequently feels forgotten. The water representing authentic spirituality given by Jesus will never dry up. As Jesus told her, this

---

[78] John 4: 1-15.

kind of authentic spirituality comes "gushing up inside that person, giving eternal life."[79] This "water of life"[80] is always present, perhaps diminished at times, but can be known as existing since life still seems more real than before.

18

Spiritual disconnections and philosophical distances are relatives to each other. It is possible to separate the two. Spiritual connections and philosophical nearness are impossible to separate, because these two relatives belong with each other. They are at home with each other.

19

Identity is not chosen by using free will. However, we also become our identity through career choices and by social influences. An aspect of that *becoming* fits well with personality abilities and skill sets. Identity is to be identified. Identity for each person has its locus in idiosyncratic traits, expressed through personality, irrespective of feelings. We become who we are therefore. Traits and abilities become a part of the constant familiarity of the self of who we are as an identity and think of them as normal and natural. Abilities and identity will not contradict each other; it fits with personality when it works effectively and for a positive benefit for society and personal existence.

20

There is an inherent need to understand the knowledge about ourselves, what we are all about, because of the power that influences

---

[79] Ibid, v.14.

[80] The phrase "water of life" is a common and I borrow it from the Scots, referring to "Single Malt Scotch" as the world's favorite whisky.

who we have become. That understanding literally turns knowledge of the self into an authoritative force where abilities and some eccentricities begin to work for the person and not against that person, nor against others. Peace is what satisfies because there is an authentic self of expression.

21

We do not notice all at once personality eccentricities and traits, identifiers, for some will be positive and others negative. Being stubborn or loving often in the same breath. The Christian learns to deal with these pieces of personality, and transform them much like converting weaknesses into strengths, as Paul instructs in the New Testament. This transformation is worked at day after day through the power of word association. The Christian can choose positive deep probing words that specify and signify a different direction on how to live with themselves and with others. What is further going on here is the work of the Spirit of God to produce worthwhile results. God first looks for results within personality, not just, how good a person can be.

22

Trusting in God helps in tenuous and awkward circumstances. Occasionally, tenuous and awkward circumstances are the only practice time that can be done effectively for any circumstance. We are not constantly on top of things. However, the more competent a person is in a particular task and trusting and depending on God, should not be self-critical. Not to know better is as a child, so the trust in God is as a child. However, to grow spiritually with experience with God's help, is to be more independent, because maturity and wisdom teach what to think and how to act. Therefore, the more competent a person is the less self-critical. Prayer for assistance, then, is less necessary. God understands and expects our independence.

23

A difficulty Christian spirituality contends with is the Christian, not the spirituality. This happens because of improved sense as a changed person into a new being or new self, however, the old being or the old self, flares up with conflicts, conflicting interests, then, disconnections. The avoidance of chaos is to have unlimited rules to live by; rules rule. Or rather, decide to yield to either the old self or the new self. When rules rule only temporarily holds back what will fall apart. The other option is to continue falling apart by yielding to the old self, which means to be disconnected and divided within the self. Not everything about spirituality and personality fit the pieces neatly together all at once, when faith first becomes real. Confidence and self-worth from the new self, will help to deal with the difficult pieces that evidentially come together with some sense to them. The new self causes the Believer to fall together, not fall apart.

24

Where there is connection, there is direction with the affirmation that life is going, as it should and getting somewhere, where it is better than before. That is faith in God for a future, not disconnected, schizophrenic and falling to pieces on the spot, faithless. In other words, the effect of salvation has begun. The effect of salvation is designed to work toward connections that give directions throughout the Christian's lifetime. The sanctification is process of growing, is also a process that the Christian can effectually see results in their life, for practical living and for spiritual depth.

25

Making connection is about the presence of mind, the presence of being there. Connection to what is external from the self, the outside world, means consciousness of being there, also means the presence of mind. Presence is that self, being there, directly in the present moment. Presence is the self that is the soul. Presence is soul, our internal reality. Our presence is always presented. If people are self-aware of themselves, psychologically cognizant, then they are aware of their presence. Simply identify that presence as soul, the internal reality. Likely, for some people the lack of a sense of presence, means not being there, therefore, such unawareness cannot differentiate themselves as different from other material objects, since they are only a material object in physical form. For them, soul is being there, but silent or not quit alive. The Temple of Delphi has the maxim, "Know Thyself." The Greeks may have had other reasons to know themselves, however the sentiment has a universal application. To know thyself is to know thy presence. Knowing God through Jesus as a portal to know our true self is not the purpose of salvation but a consequent second order discovery.

26

The presence of the soul is the self and, the soul's desire is to learn and grow, this gives traction to the idea of soul-making. Next, since the aspect of salvation in the process of sanctification brings out better aspects of personality, is dealing with an identity to be identified with, and a character developed or cut into shape, then, soul-making is not such an irregular idea. Concepts are conceived conceptions, after all. The soul is made, made to grow, expand and inflate, through the power of the concepts of words. The meaning of the word carries ideas that the soul craves. That is a psychological and philosophical heady idea wrapped in the spirituality that is Christian. The demonic, by the way, often present themselves as unreasonable, as if soulless and wordless. What is unreasonable will not have soul, or undeveloped soul. Soul-making is a reasonable idea, with soul.

27

The eyes may be the windows of the soul, as poets like to remind us. Presence, without a doubt, is evidence that there is the soul, that each person can identify as their own; that hints to a constant familiarity deep within. Is the constant familiarity therefore, the soul, or the perception as a tool, to sense the soul is there? Soul has to mean more than the idea of perception.

The New Testament has an intriguing take on eyes. The reference about eye is about the psychological effect overall, on the person, and how to live philosophically with that effect. Eugen Peterson is spot on regarding the citation on eyes and soul. He writes, "Your eyes are windows to your body. If you open your eyes wide in wonder and belief, your body fills up with light. If you live squinty-eyed in greed and distrust, your body is a dank cellar. If you pull the blinds on your windows, what dark life you will have!"[81] What is payed attention to, there is an effect, where there is an effect, and there are consequences, with responsibilities. If there is no care as to what is taken internally, into our soul, then possibly such a person simply does not care about the deeper interests of life and thus what they are all about; worse, may have a disordered personality, even schizophrenic. To be disordered is to be disturbed, but not necessarily schizoid.

28

I want to scare off the holding power of ancestry, which, ancestors can only work with words, either written or spoken tails told about their lives. The method to scare them off is to speak back. Ancestry often first speaks through the oral, then written history, in spite of how destructive or beneficial their effect. Some things are just not worth knowing, even when it is family history. Mistaken stories abound about distant relatives; most of it is gossip. James Hillman

---

[81] *The Message*, Matthew 6: 22, 23.

sharply says that nominalism has a "logophobia" over words because "words personify" since they get personal. Therefore, he says, there's "soul in words."[82] It is not that words are alive, animated – that would stretch the metaphor – but the word with soul has power and effect to affect change. Otherwise we would not be moved by any word; nor by movies or architecture, for which, we use words to describe our emotions, or the ability to pull words out of seemingly nowhere and write them down or speak out loud. Words are pulled out from the mind to be written down. Words can be seen and not just heard. Perhaps, there is a need to have a logophobia about what people say regarding ancestors with all their insecurities and flaws. Let the past die in a bed of silent words. Is that an overreaction? Possibly, although the overreaction is not a phobia about ancestors.

29

Abraham Heschel effectively says it so well: "What do most of us know about the substance of words? Estranged from the soil of the soul, our words do not grow as fruits of insights, but are found as sapless clichés, refuse in the backyard of intelligence. To the man of our age nothing is as familiar and nothing as trite as words. Of all the things they are the cheapest, most abused and least regarded. They are the object of frequent defilement. We all live in them, feel them, think in them, but failing to uphold their independent dignity, to respect their power and weight, they turn waif, elusive – a mouthful of dust."[83] What a powerful description of the weight of words. A few paragraphs earlier, "A word detached," assures Heschel, "from the person is numb; a person detached from the word is illiterate. The very essence of prayer is in blending of the two."[84] Words bring connection to the disconnected person, estranged from their own self,

---

[82] *Re-Visioning Psychology*, context, pp.8-10.
[83] *Man's Search For God*, p.25.
[84] Ibid, p.24.

then, from other people. We piece together identity with personality with the presence as soul. This "blending" is the alchemy of soul-making. Soul work, definitely, works and plays with words as tools for profound soul-making. Otherwise, we will end up with a dry soul coughing up a "mouthful of dust." Then our ancestors rule from the grave.

Words Are Power Tools

1

Etymology is the factual history and story about a word. Words narrate their own stories. Words need to be listened to, or else they are content to be ignored, unused and forgotten. Words are more than just rearranged letters from the alphabet however. Words have something unique to ply their varied meanings; thereby life has depth of meaning. Words are carriers; they transport their significance for our significance.

2

Words can sound like a disaster or just the run of things, at an industrial site, than the expression of deep meaning for soul-making. Soul-making is organized confusion like some construction site with muffled noises, messy with mud and dirt and steel mixed with pieces of wood and rocks – one problem to be solved after another – not too sure, what is being built without the plans. Growing spiritually and the making of the soul with serious substance, often as wisdom and discernment wrapped in the Spirit of God, can be messy and unsettled at times. With words from the Bible and from good literature, we grow spiritually with its complemented intellectual growth, is soul-making. That is the power of words.

3

Nicodemus is chatting with Jesus over a meal. Conversation is rather deep and philosophical. Jesus mentions wind currents. The wind is not seen but its aftermath is noticed. Wind is felt. Nevertheless, in Jesus usual philosophical turn of things says, has to be the best quotable line from Jesus: "It is the same way with every person born of the Spirit."[85] The intellectual takeout, for those "born of the Spirit" will absolutely be blown around sometimes; become a bit messed up, loosened up, to be rearranged and reconstructed is the process of spiritual growth. Eventually, often more than once, life settles down and the person discovers more about their own new self because of salvation, and they get it, who they are to be. Although, "The wind blows where it wants to and you hear the sound of it," Jesus makes it clear, "but you don't know where the wind comes from or where it is going."[86] God has designs, objectives, for our lives. We may know where we have come from, but not always, where God is leading us, both for personal development as a person and what we will do with our particularities in our place in the world. What we know with certainty, the Spirit of God will move us along. The Christian is moved along where they should be, where they should be as a person in their place in the world. Enjoy the ride!

4

Words dig deep, are explosive, to extract the core meaning buried deep within personality to pull out aspects of personality that creates an improved sense of soul. As the construction site, workers dig deep to firm up the foundation, so too does serious words extract personality eccentricities, reconstruct them, making them work for a greater good.

---

[85] NCV, John 3: 1-15 for context, v.8b.
[86] Ibid, v.8.

5

Big important sounding words are big power tools to accomplish big soul work jobs. Soul work is a big job. Big words like soul, meaning, depth, presence, becoming, and interest is a small example. Possibly, any word is a power tool that captures our attention to explore below the surface of who we think we are, cannot be neglected but investigated. There is meaning between those rearranged letters from the alphabet. Identity is to be identified is about a profound search for personal definitions. It blows away preconceived notions and expectations, who we are and what our place is in the world. This is soul-making, where the substance of whatever the soul had will be augmented, and presence becomes more connected to everything we do. We put our soul, our real self into our place in the world either with God's design or without. Therefore, who a person becomes, with God's help, begins to work for them, not against them, nor against other people. That is why the personal has persona, and the personality needs a place to express itself, because presence is soul seen through the work we do. The soul is silenced because there is no personal expression.

6

Eccentricity is not exactly identical to the idiosyncratic. Eccentricity is eccentric, off center either by deliberate choice because it fits or produces satisfaction (according to that individual) or by accidental injury. The idiosyncratic is exceptional as a unique oddity, yet as a tolerable (by most) characteristic. This may exclude the savant and/or unique oddity brought on by the innocence of birth. Both the eccentric and idiosyncratic individuals are responsible to learn a habit of beneficial expression of personality therefore. This will be a demanding task for all concerned. Responsibility implies, accordingly, the ability to respond.

7

In soul-making, there is always something to overcome. It is confusing and messy sometimes, because the soul shows itself through personality fixations, disorders, rigid consciousness, along with abilities and unique skill sets – these are how the person interacts with reality in what is rigid and out of order, and, has connection to their place in the world, in mixed bag eccentric sort of meaningful way. Soul work, evidently, is not always leisurely. The reality of the external world is rules oriented, and learning only from the school of hard knocks without working with words as power tools, is a sure method, but it takes longer to catch on to weed out the bad from the good. However, the soul loves this mixed up work.

8

Soul work is caught between wet or nourishing growing times and dry or brittle destructive times. Deep soul work has wet and dry seasons where longings for philosophical answers often is lacking.

9

James Hillman specifies accurately the conditions of the soul: "Anyway, a damp soul with its sloppy thinking and gushy feelings bogs down, occludes the brightness of vision and softens the edge of decision. The dry soul reaches up, seeks illumination. It sparks with flashes of insight and quickly catches fire. And it brings light, as elder, as mentor. But wisdom seems to require some wizening."[87] He continues a bit further as if to warn, "excess wetness" points to the need to "dry out." "Too much liquid and the soul substance tends to putrefy. You feel swamped, flooded; can't get out of this mood; stagnation. Dissolved in grief, in yearning, in messy, sticky

---

[87] *The Force of Character*, p.82.

situations. Evaporation let's of steam, boils away the moisture that kept you stuck."[88] The Christian who has a soul stuck in the quagmire of their past, yearning for it to be different, better in some way, are in a damaging place. Often they cry for more spiritual water to wet the soul, when, what is crucial is to experience a dry season to clear the vision for deeper insight. Wet and dry conditions of being, is for the soul's sake, of interest: "It must dry out the freshets of naive enthusiasms and overflows of sentimentality. The dried soul has a dry sense of humor and a dry wit – sic, like a good wine."[89] Wet and dry conditions of being are essential for soul-making. The person who is crestfallen and is self-aware, more conscious as to what is going on and what they are about, they have a greater chance to "dry out" to work with words for their soul-making. This approach does not negate Jesus' words that the Believer always has a spiritual "spring of water gushing up inside" rather, Jesus is claiming that such a spring is representative for "giving eternal life."[90] That water of life is not to be confused of shifting ground of being, often because it is wet or dry.

10

Since the soul experiences wet and dry seasons, the Christian would be wise to have curiosity to ask questions. Michael Novak zeros in on the problems dealing with the questioning experience. His claim is, "Fundamentally, the drive to question is a sort of open-mouthed hunger of attending, noticing, doubting. It is not a superficial curiosity; it is a hunger to become-one-with. An ancient name for it is intentionality; it is a sort of focusing, able to change perspective, angle, direction, depth, intensity; able, too, to double back on its own operations and to alter its own performance. Indeed, its capacity to double back on itself – the capacity of the drive to question to itself – is what

---

[88] Ibid, p.83.
[89] Ibid, p.83.
[90] NCV, John 4: 14.

makes it the source of the experience of nothingness."[91] Questions as power tools use words for the "hunger of attending" to dig deep into phobic personality developments. Questions look for the leftovers of the soul due to the hard knocks of life and family history; these are connected and partly disconnected to the wet and dry seasons of the soul. The questioning experience of probing questions transcends "sloppy thinking and gushy feelings"[92] as Hillman aptly puts it.

Soul-making by questions does not attempt to diminish the soul, as Novak later avers, "We might, of course, choose to blunt the drive to question, to escape or evade it, and thus deliver ourselves over to blind compulsions, unrecognised conditioning, and the like."[93] Word tools are inherent to "the drive to question" according to Novak; as he stays on course, "Unless we choose otherwise, the drive to question is easily lost among our other human drives: for security, for status, for pleasure, for evasion. Unless enlightened by probing questions, our choices are more likely than not trapped in patterned responses, anxieties, and inhibitions. Choice and the drive to question require one another."[94] The questioning experience as a word power tool asks for options so that the dig for deeper meaning can be intentionally directed.

Novak defines his concept a little more: "The choice that one makes in the experience of nothingness is not a choice to evade that experience or to mitigate its horror. Such a choice would be a lie. It is important to base one's life upon the experience on nothingness, to continue to return to it, and never to forget it. For the experience of nothingness is a penetrating, truthful experience."[95] Questions are diagnostic power tools. Digging and loaded with power for the discovery for our reason to be. As anyone who has had their hands on a power tool understands, there must be presence of mind of being there. While cutting a piece of pipe or cut wood, being mindful not to

---

[91] *The Experience of Nothingness*, p.45.
[92] *The Force of Character.*
[93] Ibid, p.58.
[94] Ibid, p.58.
[95] Ibid, p.61.

go too far from the line can mean disastrous results. Soul work likes to see needs to be lined up. Wisdom gives direction but discernment gives aim.

11

Meanings that feed and define the soul when torn apart seek one thing: to put the soul back together, only then the person becomes satisfied with self-acceptance, which reaches back to the acceptance from God.

12

To be ruled by excess influence from our personal past, the present has hitchhiked to the ancestral historical past – with no good results. The roots of the family tree extend too far produces a disturbed existential condition of being. That is antithetical to the roots attached to Christian spirituality since its intended gaze is towards the future. Authentic Christian spirituality crackles when the past attempts to rule us, as if ancestral influences rule from the grave with greater significance. Run from it. The past often reaches too far into the present. Sometimes the spiritual family of associated Believers have a more significant connection.

13

As we grow spiritually, over time and maturation, living in own skin with our soul because of who we are as a person, becomes more deliberate.

14

Reason's power with some objectivism causes the soul to dry out, which conversely forces intellectual roots to grow deeper and spirituality firms up, not as wet with sloppy feelings. Paying attention to words, especially in dry seasons is more effective for spiritual growth than wet times, where abundance seems to overflow.

15

Attention looks for what is needed; its optics is closer to see what is out of place. Attention hunts for loose ends in personal definition and in character. Attending to, paying attention to personal calling, sent out into our place in the world. To attend is to shepherd what will nourish the soul and the reason for being, particularly in our place in the world. Identical to Michael Novak's admonishment, "the drive to question is a sort of open-mouthed hunger of attending, noticing, doubting."[96] To attend is to shepherd what will feed and sustain spiritual strength and intellectual advancement. Paying attention is shepherding with words as power tools. It allows the shepherd's authority, with a watchful eye not to be fooled by frustrations and vulnerabilities or tempted to feel as a victim.

16

Because of salvation, soul-making with spiritual depth and intellectual astuteness is incompatible with the puerile drivel posited by some Christians. It is not beneficial when the claim that cries, "More of Jesus less of me." The requirement to become as God intended, is a concept not accommodating to the "less of me" concept. With respect to becoming a person that is positively human and sanely balanced, with their spirituality and intellectuality kept intact, intimates augmentation, not depreciation, diminishment. Besides, what else is the effect of salvation given by Jesus than an improved new self as people with their own sense of worth – with an eternal life! To have

---

[96] *The Experience of Nothingness*, p.45.

Jesus is not to be less of a person. The concept of salvation, rather, has a present tense with the future in mind.

17

When the balance between spirituality and intellectuality is lost or considered not important, there is a disconnection. Spirituality becomes airy, flighty, out of touch. Then intellectuality becomes sloppy and sluggish, slushy, watered down.

18

The power tools used for Christian spirituality helps the Believer to come alive. *This kind of spirituality will never develop into less of an experience. It currently is nothing more or less, and from that condition, it will never detract from the Christian's own sense of new self.* After all, we begin to live the eternal life now, in our place in this material world.

Deal with It

1

There is a balance given between spiritual and intellectual. Which means wisdom pays attention to what is going on. The wise pay attention to details. Otherwise, our internal reality and definition of what we are all about, is cut loose by being inattentive. What is experienced is that the grasp and sense of what we are all about begins to leak out from the soul. Leakage is about insignificance, observably, to become less than before; our place in the world, sense of belonging, is lost and has less significance. Where there is a sense of imbalance and being out of place deflates the soul. A spirituality with balance inflates the soul because there is some intellectual contents put into its contexts.

The imbalance – inattentive to what we are about, and what causes the soul to leak its significance – is a philosophical difficulty about a spiritual problem. Understanding it as a philosophical difficulty about a spiritual problem, by contrast, makes it easier to deal with. Proper word power tools go a long way to sharpen attention to details, direction and aim which help to attend to proper inflation of the soul. A philosophical difficulty pays attention to the construction of the details for soul work, whereas, a spiritual problem attends to substance, content of what makes the soul be what it cannot be otherwise, at a particular stage of soul-making. The philosophical mindset attends to specify problems that deal with complicated spiritual difficulties that often are unruly, off into various interests, without much balance. Sometimes we presume difficulties are spiritual in origin, instead, what is required is a shift of perspective.

2

Part of dealing with problems of life is to integrate the metaphor from Jesus, as The Great Shepherd into our mindset. Not so much as a shepherd forcing a direction or to follow in line, as in a sycophant and fetish way, but nudging along, a little in one way and more in another. Like sheep, who meander a little here and over there, side to side. As sheep freely walk around where to eat grass, so Jesus as Shepherd nudges where the Christian could be to freely feed their soul and care for their life. It is very relaxing. The Christian mindset accepts the motif of Jesus as Shepherd, which transcend the familiar Savior and Redeemer nametags. It is an easy transition to give attention to Jesus as The Shepherd. For Christians, The Shepherd guiding through the zigzags of life gives a greater sense of being cared for with guidance for a future.

3

The practice of the shepherd herding his or her sheep is absolutely about paying attention to attend, with a laidback approach, nudging as leading when necessary. The shepherd has the authority with a watchful eye for dangers, distractions, frustrations, anxieties, and vulnerabilities. The shepherd is a powerful image, which is the image Jesus chose for himself.[97] We have extended images from the shepherd metaphor however. We have the shepherd's crook, reaching to hook from the despair of loss, a dog for protection and assistance; the nourishment from everyone's favorite is shepherds' pie. Lest we forget, often there is the shepherd (masculine) and shepherdess (feminine), which are worthy representations of the balance of power

---

[97] Only recorded in John 10: 1-18.

in authority since they care equally. Jesus as Shepherd attends to the reality of what is crucial for significance for each Christian's interest and development. Ready for trouble, shepherds are armed to go into the wild backcountry. Shepherds attend to what demands their attention. They live for it!

Jesus as The Great shepherd does not intimidate the authentic Believer; there is a tight relationship between Jesus and those that are called his sheep or followers. Jesus, all the same, refers to himself as, "the door for the sheep."[98] Jesus bluntly positions it, that he is the way through to the other side of eternity. Presenting himself as the doorway, inoffensively now known broadly as "The Way,"[99] Jesus should not be misunderstood by his own admission as only The Shepherd. The Shepherd does not take away the importance of his other titles as, Savior, Redeemer, and Friend. However, as "the door" Jesus says, "the person who enters through me will be saved and will be able to come in and go out and find pasture."[100] This verse flies in the face of constrictive and cultural Christian spirituality, and, as a general principle against any form of spirituality, that lacks freedom. As The Shepherd, Jesus provides freedom to move intellectually and discover "pasture" of good ideas that feeds, illuminates, the soul for deeper soul-making.

As Jesus pins it down a few lines further, "I am the good shepherd. I know my sheep, and my sheep know me, just as the Father knows me, and I know the Father. I give my life for my sheep. I have other sheep that are not in this flock, and I must bring them also. They will listen to my voice, and there will be one flock and one shepherd."[101] The Believer has a reciprocal intimate relationship with Jesus with that kind of experiential and practical knowing. This is to know with deep understanding that each other has recognition, regardless of

---

[98] NCV, John 10: 7. See Hebrews 13: 20 where later Christians still viewed Jesus as Shepherd. This Shepherd concept has been diminished in importance over hundreds of years.

[99] Acts 19: 9 as one instance; compare Hebrews 10: 20.

[100] NCV, John 10: 9.

[101] NCV, John 10: 14-16.

broad knowledge obtained, or the lack of it. Shepherds are usually not seen as jerks – Jesus is no exception. As The Great Shepherd concept presented from Jesus, it carries more than the shepherd motif with a crook, but has the power of the phrase, to be shepherded. Resistance does not work toward the Believer's advantage of soul-making.

4

According to James Hillman, who comments about Alfred Adler's view on what is inferiority, in that, paraphrasing Adler, Hillman says, "We grow around and live from our weak spots. . . .[that] one's soul is one's place of least resistance."[102] However, beginning the next paragraph Hillman adds, "The locus of least resistance is the course where precisely where resistance gathers in defense. Where we are most sensitive, we are most stubborn; where we are most exposed, we expend most efforts to conceal."[103] The task is to explore why there is a defensive mechanism at all. Accordingly, "Soul is made out of its own defenses." [104] If we are resisting the Spirit of God, not wanting to be shepherded, maybe we should peal back just one layer from who we think are, but cannot become, could reveal a potential that needs to be pried loose with crowbar strength, from our encrusted soul. The "place of least resistance" is our personal place within, where resistance can yield to that, which matters. That hints to the charge given to Paul from the Lord, in effect for all of us: "My grace is enough for you. When you are weak, my power is made perfect in you."[105] Such an idea is not that strange for most Believers. Resistance captures our attention to what is below the surface of the weak aspects of personality. Neglected abilities rise to be redeemed as strengths from weaknesses.

---

[102] *Healing Fiction*, p.99.
[103] Ibid, p.99.
[104] Ibid, p.99.
[105] 2 Corinthians 12: 9

5

We think there are more abilities waiting to be pried loose from deep in personality; is a mixture of wisdom with neuroticism is experienced. Emotions either push or pull us as we are, conflicted about the reality and validity of new abilities. Power tooled words as *vulnerability, relaxed wise caution, attending to,* push and pull sensations with resistance or with pleasure. There are divided interests, obligations to consider if further pursuit of an ability requires more schooling and honing of skills, and the off chance of making a fool of one's self for thinking a new ability was possible.

6

Through actions, self-esteem is acquired. Self-esteem is initially obtained ineptly tumbling through actions, by awkward experiences, but only by doing something. Self-esteem is never acquired by the steam of willpower, nor by, not making mistakes. Rather, by practice, doing something over and over, doggedly, repetitive regardless of mistakes reveals characteristics of the soul, too. There is no such thing as halfway self-esteem; you have it or you do not. Is auto-, self-esteem ever acquired by smooth sailing? Sure, however, there will be greater second-guessing.

7

The overly confident person, usually unwise, may simply bulldoze forward without much forethought.

8

The Christian stands out from their nothingness and existential neediness, to become what God intended for them to be. Using word power tools, work the courage to stand out, to be *outstanding.*

Paul Tillich deals with that word power tool, in his philosophical existential theology. Moreover, for theology to be worth its salt should have a philosophical lean however dealing with the essence of existence. Tillich gives a slight glance for a definition of what it means *to exist*, from "Latin *existere*, 'to stand out.'" [106] It means is to stand out from our sense of non-being and nothingness. As Tillich puts it, we stand out from our "Potential being before it can come into actual being." [107] We stand out, then, to be outstanding at what we can be as a person competent with some skill sets, abilities, to become *that* person even God can appreciate. To stand out from what we were standing in, is the unfinished, disconnected soul and unknown personal abilities. Such a method advances the person to become what God has intended, as more finished than before with a connected soul to personality and identity and character. For the Christian, to be outstanding is close to, if not identical with, the concept advanced by Jesus about the ultimate meaning of life. Jesus as The Shepherd of his sheep (Believers) will have "life in all its fullness" because as Jesus pins it down, he can give a unique kind of eternal life: "I came to give life"[108] which can affect every aspect of personal life, reaching into perceived personas, including facades, for changes. So, standing out from what is incomplete means to transcend the superficial, but with a depth that reaches into soul-making.

Tillich writes, to be "outstanding" is to be "standing out of the average level of things or men, being more than others in power and value."[109] The word "average" has an intriguing etymology. It traces back to an extra charge regarding the shipment of goods, as an alteration of the equal payment of a damaged product. What is average is not over and above the price for shipping. The extra on the bill of lading has been averaged out to make things equal or better than before. Since, therefore, a person remains average;

---

[106] *Systematic Theology*, vol.2, p.20
[107] Ibid, p.20.
[108] NCV, John 10: 10
[109] *Systematic Theology*, vol.2, p.20.

they do not have a greater definition of themselves. The person who remains damaged, moreover, by not becoming more than they could be otherwise, they are average. Everyone that is maturing can identify with such a transition. That is normal; to resist growing is not normal.

The Believer, as Tillich says, stands out from "mere potentiality and has become actual"[110] they transcend the averageness of what they were naturally born. The Christian has the self-worth and self-esteem, but also to be confident about it, to embrace the potential to stand out into a better future, moving away from their neurotic existential unredeemed old self with its used-up past. Positive power tool words help the Christian to reach for that future condition of being with an identity pieced together, fuller, more satisfied life (harks back to Jesus).

9

Words as power tools to help the Christian to be outstanding as a person ought to be: *new self, salvation, to be strong, courage, faith, renewed mind, self-esteem, confidence* – these words are tools that provide a philosophical shift on how the Christian can see themselves as being able to experience their potential being.

10

The Christian stands out from the power of sin, the estrangement and disconnection, that prevented soul work and from getting to know themselves with greater or deeper meaning. Paul Tillich reminds us, after all, that we stand out of our human dilemma, not the kind God has for himself. Unlike God, we contend with "a split in reality between potentiality and actuality. This is the first step toward the rise of existentialism."[111] God has provided a way to bridge that split

---

[110] Ibid, p.21.
[111] Ibid, p.21.

and heal the distance between God only for the person who chooses to believe. Tillich then goes on to explain about God, "His existence, his standing out of his essence, is an expression of his essence. Essentially, he actualizes himself. He is beyond the split."[112] The reason why we as humans can be disconnected, spit and estranged from our self is that we are human with the propensity to sin and be unwise.

11

Christian spirituality has a *have-yet* characteristic to it. The Christian does *have* a real experience, although inherent to its characteristic is a *yet* experience: they have begun to life their potentials but have yet to experience the fulfillment of their potentials. This means to have what it takes to be spiritually minded. The knowhow to master a skill is limited, sort of living in a perpetual potential. The potential abilities are there, but have to be practiced. It is a mean, unsatisfactory, time to live with a perpetual potential. The spiritual trek is not on the fast track.

12

Experience produces a relaxed wise caution. Because of experience, we can be relaxed about what we are doing, although wise enough to be cautious. Therefore, experience brings familiarity, as much as possible, is trusted.

13

Paul told Believers to emulate other Believers. However, we do not toss aside our intelligence and wisdom, nor our own experiences. Nevertheless, let us not be too fast and throw away what we suspect is worthwhile. Paul also included a caveat: rather, emulate, "copy those

---

[112] Ibid, p.23.

who live the way we showed you."[113] Likewise, he speaks openly that these Believers must beware of the opposite, since, "Many people live like enemies of the cross of Christ."[114] Namely, it is safe to say such people "think only of earthly things"[115] therefore the bottom line is, "In the end, they will be destroyed."[116] Some people are not worth being with, nor is character worth it. In addition, we do not want to be with them when their end arrives – you know, collateral damage. Ultimately, rather, Paul means their final eternal situation.

14

The relaxed wise caution means there is enough learning, practical experience, yet, wisdom enough to be cautious, since anything can happen. Perhaps too the relaxed wise caution is where, as it were, the person steps back and bracket off, compartmentalize themselves from what is going on around them. Peter Koestenbaum says, "To bracket (or to 'thematize') is to take a phenomenon out of the stream of experience and examine it in isolation."[117] He uses the example of photography that captures (brackets off) the image of a subject for study. "Reality is left intact. It is only our observation that is added to it. Changes are made only in the mind,"[118] adds Koestenbaum. However, for Koestenbaum there is another level, "Reduction means to reflect on experience rather than to participate in it."[119] What he means is that, "In fact, the word *reduction* means in Latin to lead back or to step back."[120] It does not mean to lean back, rather to "lead" yourself back, therefore to step backwards, not by another, but by

---

[113] NCV, Philippians 3: 17.

[114] Ibid, v.18.

[115] Ibid, v.19.

[116] Ibid, v.19.

[117] *The New Image of the Person*, p.33.

[118] Ibid, p.33.

[119] Ibid, p.34.

[120] Ibid, p.34.

one's own self, leading one's self. Accordingly, to step back is similar to the relaxed wise caution where we have experience with what requires a cautious action, however we are relaxed about it because in the mind, theoretically, we have stepped back to examine the situation. Otherwise, we could become excessively and emotionally involved, unable to be wise. Stepping back to think allows time. Time, then, makes it possible not to be fooled, by people pretending who they are not. In addition, there is time to inspect concepts for their authority and authenticity, for implications in practical life.

Again, to Koestenbaum, "Reflexive thinking, on the other hand, is consciousness turned back upon itself. Reflexive thought is uniquely philosophical. It is self-referential; it is not the act of consciousness but of self-consciousness. Reflexive thought is infinite regress. It is thought thinking about thought."[121] From that vantage point, we stop, we wait, and we cogitate, since we have applied a relaxed wise caution as deep reflexive thinking before we act or before we believe – anything. We do not want to be reactive every time. Koestenbaum mentions that such an approach is "philosophical." Philosophy at its roots is more phenomenological and existential; therefore, it can be apprehended, as *doing philosophy* is a way of life. Doing philosophy is not just mental gymnastics. Perhaps that is why some Christians are at home wrestling with philosophical ideas, hunting for the practical application of ideas and beliefs. What Koestenbaum has to teach is that the hunt can be effectively directed and less aimless.

15

Christian spirituality contains enough freedom to hang itself. What does that mean? Is too much freedom negative and destructive? No. How we use the freedom we have as Christians does matter. It matters to use wisdom and common sense, as needed. We can turn our spirituality into a license to do whatever the rule of what

---

[121] Ibid, p.35.

is good and acceptable. The result is, often mistakenly so, to always be good and acceptable. This license turns spirituality into a burden where rules rule. On the other side, is the comparable extreme, where excessive societal practices and conventions, have its own burdens where rules rule. Frequently this *makes* things function. Often, however, as rules rule, it kills the freedom of spirituality. To function in society requires the skill to walk on a sword's edge; fall and you will be philosophically split and be spiritually numb. Next, spiritual growth or depth and intellectual astuteness has ceased. Freedom can be utilized through rules to restrict actions, when not necessary, which ends deep growth as a person. Freedom used to remain on a plateau spiritual level not going anywhere further becomes viable; or becomes a dead end cul-de-sac experience. The erroneous use of freedom ends free expression as a person and then the proverbial wall has been hit; hard knocks brings life to a point for reassessments. Often then, some hit that wall hard enough and use their freedom to give up on God and become a Christian drop out.

16

For some, a plateau experience in spirituality can have this odd arrival feel to it. Arrival in spirituality has stability because it actually has achieved maturity, yet, there is a doubt in the stability. Why does doubt show up while on a plateau spiritual arrival experience? Doubt, however, is not dangerous or a sin, nor is the questioning experience. The doubt about arriving at a level of spiritual stability or maturity is flawed reasoning since it resists conclusions. On a plateau experience, doubt creates the feel of being stuck – turn around and go back to less depth, or stay put for what comes next, is anyone's guess. Right here, at that "creates the feel" point, is where the God from Nietzsche can die a quick death. Many Believers become *un*-Believers. Born again skeptics and born again agnostics become the uncommitted discontents – they are not committed to the old familiar run of things spiritually that got them to the arrival of the plateau experience. They may assert confidently as to echo Poe's raven, "nevermore." Such previous Believers become the bored again with the entire Christian spiritual meaning as the reason for being.

17

The spiritual plateau arrival of maturity can cause some to presume they are out of sync, not in proper relationship with God. This is imaginative unwise conjecture based on wrongheaded thinking and combined with feelings. It is a philosophical wild idea that claims the relationship with God is negative from the ground up. The Believer's relationship with God is never negative. The plateau arrival has the certainty of spiritual maturity with an intellectual astuteness; has been achieved with soul-making. That perceptive concept has somehow slipped out of sight. An experience in the arrival condition of being, must not be precluded that nothing more has yet to be spiritually experienced – as if nevermore.

That "nevermore" comes deep from the hollow throated voice of doubt. This kind of plateau experience turns into a cul-de-sac, where spirituality can be numbed senseless and ultimate love is a loveless dead end. Right here, at that point, – the love of knowledge and the love of understanding regarding spiritual truths – can become cold hard data. What we know and understand becomes stuff stuffed into the head without reaching the soul. Moreover, perchance, experience obtained so far, may itself get in the way. Further possible experiences will be compared with previous experiences. Comparisons to other experiences lead to more possible new advanced spiritual insight, which is doubted. Sometimes we grow so far in depth, insight, wisdom and discernment, yet, not remain open as we once were. Here too, some cease to believe in God. Like Icarus in Greek myth, freely flew too high towards the light and heat of the sun, against wiser advice. The wax melted holding the feathers together, and Icarus freely fell to his death. Flying high spiritually, only to fall like Icarus. The use of freedom, to not use freedom, brings a freefall. Illumination, although, needs a relaxed wise caution. It is wiser to wait on the plateau level of spiritual maturity, as if before the Lord. Perhaps wisdom tells us arrival, ultimately in this lifetime, is for another time of fuller life. Wait this event out; do not be like Icarus who fell to his death.

18

I managed to do what most Christians would not dare. Unlike Icarus falling in the Greek narrative, however, I listened to the feminine power of wisdom. For approximately five years, I stopped reading my Bible. Holy of horrors! Honestly, I sort of stopped reading. I never picked up the Bible unless to check on something. Life went on as expected – trusting God and praying as usual. Relationship with God remained the same, namely, nothing was out of sync, because I have a relationship with God, not a book about God. Guilt for not reading the Bible never enters my consciousness. I was not surprised about that perspective.

I have read the *Revised Standard Version* for about 50 years. During this sabbatical from regular, nearly daily Bible reading, I did read a little from those handy devotional books. I did not dislike the Bible. However, it simply became, not boring, but tiresome. It became tiresome in a sort of common ordinary way. The feel of reading it was that I nearly knew what was coming next; been there, done that.

Meanwhile, reading those often insightful devotionals, I'll never forgot a line about being legalistic, or something like it, where hand-me-down written texts can be so much with so little substance, as if rules rule kind of mindset. The succinct sentence, convinced, perhaps Eugene Peterson pins it: "Printers ink became embalming fluid." That is a line that sticks as an intellectual butt kicker. After five years of no consistent Bible reading, the insight was, because I read an older version. I needed to discover a more recent Bible version. Upgrade, not downsize my reading. Could it be, that deliberate and simple? It was. Sometimes I can be a bit slow on the draw.

Already knew the history about the Bible: manuscripts, translations verses versions, and what a decent study Bible was like. I searched the Internet to read different Bible versions. I settled with the *New Century Version*. It is an exceptional reading encounter, almost like the meeting of two minds. I read that version for a number of years. Eventually, after a few more years, I settled on the *English Standard Version*. Since its predecessor is the RSV, enjoyed reading it, however, quote more from the NCV. Too often, we can doggedly read the Bible and it is too familiar, then we can become tired of it. What happens is some erroneously think their relationship with God is out of sync, whereas all that is required is a different Bible version, preferably a worthwhile study Bible. Wisdom tidbit: I never, as long as I have been a Christian, presume my relationship with God is constructed on the negative.

19

The act of reading, however done without the soft love of insight, will turn that reading event into an acid dripping through the soul. The love is gone. Words as power tools have lost their power. Conversely, when reading, where knowledge is complemented with understanding, not stuff stuffed into the head like data mining, then there is spiritual nourishment for the soul. Epistemology is about the justification of knowledgeable truths, which seeks to acquire reasonable understanding of that knowledge. There is more to knowledge than stuff stuffed into the head, understanding goes deeper to the soul. In spirituality, the attempt is to acquire knowledge but to have understanding is an acknowledgement, which provides nourishment for the soul. It's not complicated; but thinking is a necessity. Otherwise, Bible reading with study is a waste of life. Roots for spiritual meaning will not go deep, and meaning is uprooted.

20

Jesus told some religious leaders that eternal life is not secured by the act of reading and by studious effort. He is specific: "You carefully study the Scriptures because you think they give you eternal life. They do in fact tell about me, but you refuse to come to me to have that life."[122] Still, we know insights can reveal a deeper spirituality; that indicates the reader is open to truth, here about Jesus.

21

Reading material about spiritual interests is a tightrope initiative to give in, to God, without the need to give up. Reading the Bible is, as though it is reading you back, and giving in to that effect, without losing. It is unwise to presume the Bible, or better, the Spirit, is not in fact reading you through the power of words. The Spirit has a way of getting around our defenses, poking holes into closeted beliefs, even weird beliefs, so that we deal with soul work. We give in without the need to give up. Accordingly, we are convinced to be convicted to be converted.

22

Right out from the chute, in John's gospel, he speaks unequivocally, but to anyone who pays attention: "In the beginning there was the Word. The Word was with God, and the Word was God. He was with God in the beginning."[123] God did not send to humankind a book. God sent his Word commonly acknowledged as Jesus the Christ. Moreover, that Word as Jesus is not printer's ink. Jesus is the concept of God made visible.

23

We slow down in order to stop, instead of hitting the proverbial wall hard and fast. The Psalmist chisels the idea into our minds

---

[122] NCV, John 5: 39, 40. The ESV has "you think that in them you have eternal life."

[123] NCV, John 1: 1, 2. Compare Colossians 1: 15 for an agreement between two writers.

to its essence: "I find rest in God: only he can save."[124] Spiritual language uses word power tools, such as *stop*, or *relaxes* – "rest" is the biblical word. But, that rest must be *found*. "I find rest," he says, in the presence of God. Later on Jesus stretches what the Psalmist said by stating it more concisely. Jesus tells more, what is implied: "Come to me, all of you who are tired and have heavy loads, and I will give you rest."[125] Sick and tired of the psychobabble and the philosophical primitive answers; crave a relieve from one constant problem to solve after another – Jesus is saying he "will" help to deal with it, the heavy lifting will be shared; maybe you're also lifting things that are best left alone. Not to be outdone, likewise, the writer of Hebrews borrows from Jesus and the Old Testament, explains the concept further, "We who have believed are able to enter and have God's rest."[126] Such a spiritual kind of rest can be found and the Believer is "able to enter" as if relaxed in peace.

24

God is not about to have a relationship with anyone if it is forced, command a lockstep jackboot, walk the line. Nor is such a relationship so tight nothing can pry the Believer away from God. The reality is, all the same, some people are pried loose from the relationship with God, because of freedom. Love, indeed, is not enough because some people's needs require attention to mental health and material blessings. The assurance, however, is that God will never abandon a Believer. However, God will leave them alone, if that is what the person desires. The New Testament author of Hebrews borrows from an Old Testament verse: "I will never leave you; I will never abandon you."[127] The confidence of such love fills the soul, as if to

---

124 NCV, Psalm 62: 1.
125 NCV, Matthew 11: 28.
126 NCV, Hebrews 4: 3a.
127 NCV, Deuteronomy 31: 6 citation for this Hebrews 13: 5 reference.

claim ultimate connection in a relationship. Confidence pours in and fills the soul; nothing is wasted.

25

The persuasion from God that he will not abandon the Christian is implied throughout the New Testament, although not specified as Hebrews 13: 5 assures. Jesus, however in John's account, does not nail it exactly, but has an exception clause as to what he means by him not leaving the Christian. After assuring them that "another Helper [Counselor or Comforter] to be with you" he nonetheless insists: "I will not leave you all alone like orphans; I will come back to you."[128] Jesus recognizes "not leave you" as a material fact, although there is the possibility that Christians will not be "alone like orphans." Orphans do not have parents; at best, they have guardians as helpers. If the Spirit, the Helper is always present, what does the orphan metaphor infer? Does it mean the Christian will never be left alone, but not as an orphan? Left alone, not as an orphan, except occasions where God seems distant, not due to the Christian being distant towards God, nevertheless, is a separation without the indifference of estrangement. What we have from Jesus is, "I will not leave you" but at times sense of being left out just, "alone like orphans." Not to acknowledge that at times Christians have tacit curiosity about God's distance; yet calmly assured, ultimately, distance is not being left all alone all the time, nor is it complete abandonment as from a careless parent.

It is no exaggeration, to go on, some Christians are acquainted with God taking a few steps back, away, from their lives. Historically, such people have been accused of heresy, tortured and killed, sold into slavery – occasionally by Christians. Today, Christians are killed what some refer as the Islamonazi. Christian girls given or sold as sex slaves, human trafficking. Has God stepped out and gone somewhere?

---

[128] NCV, John 14: 16, 17.

Fortunately, God will "never leave you" has the "never" as the ultimate permanent assurance. No doubt, that is the point. Poe's raven calls again, "nevermore." One thing for sure, there is no more ever, in never. Perhaps God ultimately leaves a person, in the case of apostasy. Even in apostasy situation, it is difficult to out-guess how God would play it out, if the fallen returns.

26

The Bible[129] informs finding God and pleasing God is possible. Lurking behind this Bible reference in Hebrews, is a connection and disconnection regarding, not so much faith, but relationship with God. A particular Believer already has faith to "please God" for it implies (11: 6) that is the situation. Let's say such a Believer has faith, but no real good deeds to speak of and whatever relationship they may have with God, if any, is surface, without deep life altering effect; either agnostic or deistic to the grave. Such a Believer has a connection to the *idea of God* but disconnected to God personally. God is more like *The Friend*. God may possibly be amused by such a Believer's lack of seriousness "to find him" in a deeper relationship.

Meanwhile, another Believer has discovered a deeper authentic sense of knowing God. However, they caught on that a personal relationship has the knowledge to understand what it is like to feel the distance of God. Whereas the loose ended Believer, thinks God's distance is normal because God is not personal, not an intimate knowable God. God is a force without persona. Therefore, such a Believer usually does not experience personality-altering events. Spiritual experiences are rare and soul-making is an idea avoided.

Believers, wisely, who have a personal relationship with God and experience the possibility of God's distance, view it as abnormal or disliked, since they recognize the existential angst that later comes as inertia and feelings of being forgotten. If the loose-ended Believer

---

[129] Hebrews 11: 6.

does not know better, God's distance seems normal because they never have been close to God. Some other Believers get it, that God and themselves are friends, have a functional relationship, although there's more of an intimate relationship, despite the odd distant feel that comes with an authentic friendship; both know there's more to it than friendship, but a Savior shepherd relationship.

27

Not only is Jesus the *Savior, Shepherd,* but through the Spirit a *Helper.* Each of these nametags refers to *advocate.* Anyway, known as Messiah, declared Son of God by the angel Gabriel; teacher and healer, a carpenter of a sort, and knew when wine is made it should be considered very good.[130] Accordingly, Jesus must have drank some good wine. Moreover, anticipating the future paparazzi, Jesus' character was maliciously maligned, alleged to have drunk too much wine and hung around the wrong crowd.[131] That allegation of drinking too much and hanging around "those people" never stuck to Jesus. Nowadays worse revisionist, want to *suggest* Jesus had a wife. Let us see now, Jesus as Savior, Shepherd, Helper, and Friend, isn't enough nametags. Revisionism becomes puerile and boring.

28

As expressed in the melancholic sound from the much-loved song, "What A Friend We Have In Jesus" may not go far enough. Joseph Scriven,[132] who immigrated to Canada from Ireland, wrote it first as a poem in 1855. His life is a fascinating study of psychological pain. As we now know, the song is from anguished experience, rejection and disappointment. The song, nonetheless, has influenced many

---

[130] A short list, Isaiah 9: 5-7; John 4: 26; Matthew 8: 1-17; Luke 1: 29-35; John 3: 2; 13: 13; Matthew 13: 55; John 2: 1-11; Matthew 11: 19.
[131] Matthew 11: 19.
[132] Wikipedia.org.

to accept Jesus as Savior. In the Bible, Jesus is never given the title "Friend." Jesus did refer to his Followers at one point as "friends" instead of "servants."[133] Jesus as "The Friend" evolved decades after the New Testament was written. The sentiment is intimated but not absolutely stated in Scripture. Nowadays Jesus as "Friend" common usage among Christians. Early Christians perhaps used the word "Friend" sparingly when signified to Jesus and God as such. It was an overlooked opportunity to use a word that Jesus introduced. The word "Friend" used for Jesus, all the same, is an effective word power tool. The early Christians did not pick up that tool, to take advantage of. A slight off mention of being a friend to God that involves an active relationship shows up years later, in a notation about Abraham's faith earned him that status.[134] There is a chance by inference in the New Testament; Christians too can have such status with God, as friends.

29

Jesus does consider his Followers as friends, however, he also expects his friends to do what he taught. Jesus has some conditions for friendship – no fuzzy-feel-good ideas from the Son of God. There is no such thing as unconditional love; always a clause, a reason and stipulation attached; even from God. God expects loyalty and faith, character and friendship, so that a true authentic relationship does not work against each other. The Christian looks for more than a friend in Jesus however.

---

[133] John 15: 12-17.
[134] James 2: 20-23.

DEAL WITH IT, AGAIN

1

More than a Friend: Savior. The purpose of salvation is to secure eternal life that is connected with God because of Jesus. That connection is a personal functional relationship to bring out better aspects of personality, which is a spiritual healing affecting who the Christian is as a person. The person who becomes a Christian has the opportunity to explore the potentialities of their personality that were hidden or unknown. This is the process of soul work that produces soul-making. Soul work, works with word power tools, namely from Bible study and from extra-biblical literature. A significant part of that retooling of reading some new words that exceeds mere reading to stuff the head with knowledge, but acquire understanding to become an authentic person. Not because of psychotherapy as such, rather due to a spiritual wakening by the Spirit of God; have consequences for practical living, pleasing life for God and for oneself.

The Savior Jesus saves, delivers, rescues, makes life whole-*some*, that gives a chance to start over, clean and new. The Savior Jesus offers rescue from the personal destruction of existential ruin and spiritual death, which is a numbed feeling about deeper meaning. Here is when personal abilities covered over in a dark past – regardless of how much enlightenment is presumed to have obtained – becomes to be more interesting in plain view: salvation encourages to deal with personal calling, a reason for being, in our place in the world. There is a future. The author (probably Luke) of Acts says, "Jesus is the One whom God raised to be on his side, as leader and Savior. Through him, all the people could change their hearts and lives and have their sins forgiven, [as well]."[135] Later Paul writes, "For this end we toil and strive, because we have our hope set on the living God, who is the Savior of all people, especially of those who believe."[136] Jesus is the Savior as God is the Savior. Then John echoes himself, but improves on Paul's idea, "That which was from the beginning, which we have heard, which we have seen with our own eyes, which we looked upon and have touched with our hands, concerning the word of life."[137] Jesus is that "word of life" not material letters rearranged from the alphabet, nor literally as in the Eucharist, which only symbolizes Jesus for who he is.

2

More than a Friend: Shepherd. In a general overview, the ideas about a shepherd have been dealt with in the chapter "Deal with It" in sections 2 and 3. Namely in section 3, is averred, "Jesus as The Great shepherd does not intimidate the authentic Believer; there's a tight relationship between Jesus and those that are called his sheep or followers." Jesus says it himself, "I am the good shepherd."[138] As The Shepherd, Jesus is not the wrong shepherd, nor the wannabe shepherd attempting a mediocre job; rather he is good at what he does. In effect, at self-promotion, Jesus is saying, "I'm the guy!" It is difficult to image a shepherd as a jerk, somebody who does not care. The fact that Jesus is upfront with his intentions indicates not all shepherds are equal. The shepherd's intent is to attend to, tending, to be watchful with resolve to direct and guide with careful attention and authority. The shepherd has presence.

Jesus as The Shepherd has presence. Jesus attends to what *needs* attention. Attention is given for the *need* to *experience* the event of

---

[135] NCV, Acts 5: 31.
[136] ESV, 1 Timothy 4: 10. Compare John 4: 42; Acts 13: 23, 27.
[137] ESV, 1 John 1: 1. Compare 2 Timothy 1: 10.
[138] NCV, John 10: 14a.

salvation. That has as an inherent affect to encourage insight into personality developments with the *need* for significance and the *need* for soul-making. This Shepherd attends to many needs! The Christian's mindset is, as they walk around in daily life, there is The Shepherd's attention for their care, watching over them, thereby, the thought that a future will improve is highly probable. There is a *have-yet*[139] mindset entrenched within Christian spirituality, since it has a future to offer now and yet to come. That means Christians can enjoy being shepherded by their personal Shepherd, who cares for their souls. Moreover, well-being is not such an odd stretch, as it assures the Christian; Jesus is "the Shepherd and Overseer of your souls."[140] Christians have the confidence and self-esteem to live beyond their possibilities that are potentiality into actualities.

3

More than a Friend: Helper. The helper is very close to the idea of what a friend is, except the latter may only go so far because of conflicting obligations. The helper or worker is paid for what they do. Either way, the helper brings support and assistance, the right-hand person for the right job. The person who is a helper pays attention, has a sharp eye for the interest for the other person needing the care for the help.

The familiar and loved quotation by many Christians is from Jesus, "If you love me, you will obey my commands. I will ask the Father, and he will give you another Helper to be with you forever – the Spirit of truth. The world cannot accept him, because it does not see him or know him. But you know him, because he lives with you and he will be in you. I will not leave you all alone like orphans."[141]

---

[139] See chapter "Christian Spirituality," sec.31; "Deal With It," sec.11.

[140] NCV, 1 Peter 2: 25. Compare Hebrews 13: 20b, 21a, "God raised from the dead our Lord Jesus Christ, the Great Shepherd of the sheep, because of the blood of his death" that "began the eternal agreement with God" for all who believe.

[141] NCV, John 14: 15-18. Compare John 15: 26, 27; 16: 7-11; Ephesians 1: 13, 14; 1 John 2: 1.

Interestingly, Jesus reminds his Believers they already knew this Helper since that Helper "lives in you." Jesus and the Helper are one and the same, only that, when Jesus will not be with them physically, the Helper's presence will become more evident. These Believers, by extension all future Believers, are assured they will not be forgotten and the evidence will be the acquired better ideas of truth regarding the things Jesus taught. From that evidence from the Helper, it is not an exaggeration that new Believers would discover profound spiritual insight, characteristics of wisdom and discernment about spirituality from God.

The word power tool "Helper" often is translated "Counselor" or "Comforter" borrowing from the Greek. The idea stems from the words *parakletos* to denote the Spirit as Comforter. That reaches back to *paraklesis* to describe the concept of giving comfort or good consolation. Hence, *para* means to *be called beside* or *along by the side*, as a paralegal conducts help as an advocate of law. The paramedic person assists, is along by the side of doctors. The "para" archetype or model works effective as a power tool to indorse the word *paraword* (my word). A paraword is any word that works with another causing it to be more effective, convincing. Anyway, what Jesus is telling us, the Helper or Advocate and himself, are the same. When the Christian is counseled (example of a paraword) by the Helper, who is the Spirit of God, Jesus comforts them, as well. The idea intimates that the Spirit of God is malleable in the sense of adjusting to our situations, just as a shepherd does to the need of his sheep.

Jesus as the Helper through the Spirit, also intimates that the Christian is to be influenced, better yet, to be led, guided and directed but not in a forceful way, by God. To repeat Jesus, "If you love me, you will obey my commands." Yet, in the previous verse (14) he said, "If you ask me for anything in my name, I will do it." Therefore, there appears to be a bit of give and take, although Jesus assures proper help is a given or prearranged. What is this being led about, what does it look like in practical life? Led by Jesus, as Shepherd is identical to being helped by the Helper. The Helper guides and directs.

Without getting too far in the tall grass of confusion, however, a person under the influence of drugs or adult beverages is not guided by the Helper. The Spirit leads the Christian in an open format or style, working with our personality. Paul, however, specifies what it means, deliberately and consciously, when the Spirit can lead, "Do not be drunk with wine, which will ruin you, but be filled with the Spirit."[142] Obviously we cannot prohibit the use of some medications that produce a drowsy effect or under anesthesia or the simple act of sleeping or daydreaming – any loss of consciousness *may* not produce the Spirit's ability to lead the Christian. The point is, Christians desire the Helper to assist them as it is necessary, however under a destructive or unproductive influence does not help to be guided by the Spirit.

4

To be spiritually minded, cognizant why we do what we believe and what is going on around us, is to have a sense of being grounded, stable and secure, as a person who enjoys being shepherded, guided and directed by God. This also conveys encouragement of Jesus as a Friend, but more as a Savior, Shepherd, and Helper. The paraword attached to Jesus as a Friend; likewise as a Savior, Shepherd, and Helper, is the word power tool, *Anchor*. The nautical anchor metaphor keeps such titles of Jesus integrated into Christian spirituality. The anchor also *helps*, for our personal identity and character to be anchored, not tossed around as though listing unbalanced.[143] Without the mindset that integrates the anchor, spirituality has the tendency to be all over the place, and becomes airy, flighty, off the wall aberrant thinking cannot be substantiated where experiences of discovery and illumination become more important than content

---

[142] NCV, Ephesians 5: 18. Compare Titus 1: 7, seems to intimate also, leaders show by example how much to drink, if to show "not to drink too much."

[143] See, Ephesians 4: 14, 15, "tossed about like a ship. . .trying to fool us. . .[but] we will grow up in every way in Christ."

of spirituality. The paraword anchor helps to hold, coherence with stability as a mindset.

The metaphor of the anchor works in the background of what Jesus has accomplished in the soul and personality of the person who has become a Christian. The only locus in Scripture, of Jesus as The Anchor blended with the effect of The Anchor for confidence and holding power, style and encouragement, is in Hebrews: "We have this hope as an anchor for the soul, sure and strong. It enters behind the curtain in the Most Holy Place in heaven, where Jesus has gone ahead of us and for us."[144] The anchor (Jesus) is dropped to hold us secure (anchored) spiritually with intellectual astuteness, not psychotic in useless anxiety, but affirmed in personality and character. Holding on for dear life with faith alone, needs to be anchored in Jesus. To be anchored, secured, as a package deal as to who Jesus is as Savior, Shepherd, and Friend, along with Jesus as The Anchor makes soul work possible.

There is a play on the word anchor in these verses. Anchor also means God's "promise" (verse 17) is true for God's "purposes" (verse 18) which is "this hope" (verse 19). That sort of anchors "encourages us who came to God for safety" (verse 18). Jesus as Anchor anchors the hope for security, as the "anchor for the soul" so that the Christian becomes "sure and strong." In a way, there is no indifference to the nautical anchor. When stationary or dropped, it conveys the power it holds. Shopping malls ("temples of modern pleasure," some brag) have their anchor stores designed to attract shoppers to meet commercial gain and meet material needs. Jesus The Anchor has effective holding power for authentic peace with God and the self. That enables the Christian have "safety."

5

The new self from the Christian spiritual experience has the sense of being sort of complete, at one with whatever is the opposite of

---

[144] NCV, Hebrews 6: 19, 20a.

themselves; yet, acknowledge that soul work means finally being pieced together with a sense of incompleteness, that we have/yet more to develop as we discover growing spiritually. Not knowing what comes next can be frustrating. One consolation: personality with identity and character is being dealt with for definition and expression of presence. Such change is not by sheer will power, self-help, but by the effect of the Spirit of God.

6

The word "character" indicates the distinctive nature of that, which is carved, and an instrument or tool for making marks like a chisel. Character is made, carved, unlike personality that seems to be there, from the beginning of personal existence. Whereas identity can take on characteristics from environment: people and places, situations, although we do have power to allow how much we will accept exterior influences to shape us. We identify with our identity, more as, an expression of personality traits. Personality has traits, has idiosyncratic personality signifiers that identifies me from you and from everyone else, either developed at birth or slightly during pregnancy.

7

Some Christians believe personality is given by God because, as it goes, so too is the soul. Nothing convinces that God hands out personalities, let alone, souls, to new babies. Otherwise, the bad seed phenomena, bad personality from the start as in sociopathy where conscience is nonexistent would not have validity – God is to blame goes the presumption. Moreover, what would be the point of blaming God? Sure, why not blame God for everything? Talk about getting a bad whack. Everything then has its antecedent existence returned to what God said and what God did. Some things just happen, with or without God.

101

8

The Psalmist writes that God has "made me."[145] The author has a good hunch God knows more than what he does, even about his own life. The Psalmist is not advocating for a universal application, however, claiming for one person (himself) they can't wrap their mind around the idea that they could not exist, if it were not for God; seems premature if not outright naïve. We have to admire his intellectual honesty that he does not know enough: "Your knowledge is amazing to me; it is more than I can understand."[146] Today we know more and have more accurate understanding about biology. The biology or chemical and molecular structure of being "made" or formed as a physical human being, is the process of self-creation. However, to claim that God participates in making each human is naïve. The Bible says that God gave plants and animals including humans to reproduce themselves.[147] Humans have the exception not to be determined by biology. Freedom and free will would mean absolutely nothing therefore. Humans can chose not to behave like an animal, or a plant for as much. To deny free will, which we can, for all purposes, is therefore to deny ourselves since we are a freedom.

9

Principles are compromised before beliefs. A compromise on principle is based upon the situation, upon specifics of the scenario, not the circumstance of a particular condition. A situation is what is going on in a particular place or period, a condition it creates is a scenario. A circumstance is what encircles, what can cause another

---

[145] NCV, Psalm 139: 14, context 13-16. Compare Jeremiah 1: 5 is not about creating Jeremiah, but his calling. It would be a stretch of proportional imagination to turn this into a universal application; no precedent. Other examples are only Jesus and John the Baptist. How they were "made" is incidental.

[146] Ibid, v.6.

[147] Genesis 1: 11, 24, 27.

cause or condition to affect a particular result. A circumstance affects a situation. A belief, as example, is that life is precious and sacred. Nevertheless, a principle will allow for defensive killing another human, not as indiscriminate murder. Abortion to save the woman's life is another example. Principles, however, can be changed or relinquished and temporarily or permanently. Principles work with freedom to use free will, whereas, beliefs will not relinquish but use freedom to be unfree for a particularity. Beliefs go deeper, transcend time and situations. Belief in God, for instance, is not a principle, but a belief. Principles guide, suggest, theorize, welcome options about truth, how to live life. Beliefs are closer to the bone, and deal with personality and identity; will be practiced, not theorized. Principles work with parawords to ratchet up word effectiveness, whereas a belief may or may not attach to a paraword.

10

How we act and react deals with awareness of freedom and how to use it, if at all. Based upon principle or belief, a curve ball is thrown, a difficulty is thrown, a decision must decide on the spot, how to deal with a situation. Therefore, if a belief is compromised over a principle, advisedly, there is a lack of standards and values. The question is: If there is compromise, can people live with themselves and will it be justified?

11

The spiritual life of soul-making deals with the split between the sense of our old self and the sense of the new self.[148] The new sense of self deals with aspects of personality definitions. Often the new self, lives with a have-yet aspect. This have-yet is a realization of greater personal improvements to be actual in the development of

---

[148] Colossians 2: 13

potentials. The sense of old self and the new sense of self are at odds. This is normal and natural part of Christian spirituality. Usually our thinking needs to catch up to the salvation experience. Such a split is philosophical about a spiritual condition of being. The split does fade, diminish, as spiritual growth matures and intellectuality advances. We learn to have a relaxed wise caution, and, we give in to the Spirit without the need to give up. That occurs as the old self is at less odds with the new self.

12

Christian spirituality seeks to deal with by mending, to repair and heal the incompleteness and the sense of being complete, spiritually. The Christian's spirituality hunger is now satisfied, meanwhile, there is the expectation there is more to it. The more to it, means to understand more about God while learning more about who we are as a person. This also explains why there cannot be spiritual growth unless there is intellectual astuteness or advancement. Anyone can advance intellectually, seems obvious, and simultaneously not grow spiritually, seems obvious as well. Christian spirituality enjoys the unique combination of being spiritual with some wise discernment. Get the mixture off, blended wrong, and end up with an impure concoction with a watered down spirituality and intellectuality. Spirituality becomes flighty and airheadish, often politically correct thinking with its close relative groupthink, but always inordinately concerned with form over substance.

13

Philosophical primitivism is rooted in the underdeveloped soul. This is evidenced as an immature spirituality, which leads to an aberrant unwise sense of aloneness, possibly feeling ignored with sense of being out of place. Other times, the philosophical primitivism is soaked in existential angst, and speculative notions whether pieces of the soul have died, or a combination with actual inferiority and estranged to that which matters. Philosophical primitivism is unhealthy!

14

It makes practical sense that soul work to get rid of useless psychic junk. We learn to let go of dying junk. The soul, our internal reality welcomes a good dying of particular pieces of the old self that works against us. Otherwise, those neurotic phobic disorders only hold us back from effective soul-making. It clears out mental space for better interests. Still, losing hurts.

15

To throw away, degrade or despise, what is incomplete, unfinished, of an ability yet to be known, is to throw away connections about who we can be and what we can accomplish as a person. Personal abilities should be pieced together, complimenting personality, as actual positive sense of completeness and perfection. When connections about perceived abilities are not actualized from potentials, there is disappointment with God and ourselves. We speculate if expectations were too unreal. However, we can get caught up, catch fire with burning insights, with new ideas attached with the new identity associated with the new self of the second birth experience. We think we can do anything. The source of such erroneous mindset is what Paul wrote while restricted in prison, "I can do all things through Christ, because he gives me strength."[149] However, the pervious sentence begins "I know how to live when,"[150] in all kinds of normal and natural conditions. Paul can be practical to conclude he has the ability (skill, aptitude) and the capability (competence, knowhow) to endure the best of times and the worst of times. Paul did follow through with,

---

[149] NCV, Philippians 4: 13.
[150] Ibid, v.12.

"But it was good that you helped me when I needed it."[151] Some things we thought were impossible or excruciatingly difficult, but have discovered with insights and practice, unknown strengths that make it possible, although we get by with a little help from friends.

16

Christians believe they can accomplish anything – with the Lord. They refer to Jesus. Jesus, concerning faith, did claim to move mountains and destroy trees, although "mountain" is used as a metaphor for existential troubles. We know that to be an accurate interpretation since Jesus himself never moved any physical mountains or rearranged landscapes. That is a no-brainer, except the sentiment literally catches fire for some adventurous enthusiasts. Jesus did say that a kind of mountain could be moved "from here to there."[152] Jesus repeated himself later on, "Go fall into the sea."[153] Rather, it would be wise to focus on the subject of faith that Jesus is actually referring to: "You people have no faith, and your lives are all wrong."[154] In the second quote Jesus tones down a bit, speaking straight, "I tell you the truth, if you have faith and do not doubt, you are able to do what I did"[155] by ending a tree's life. Faith to do what Jesus can do is not to alter the landscape. Paul even borrows the analogy from Jesus talking about mountain transplantation[156] without any evidence he ever accomplished the feat literally, nor any from the early Christians.

Jesus does push the idea elsewhere, "I tell you the truth, whoever believes in me will do the same things that I do. Those who believe will do greater things than these, because I go to the Father. . . . If

---

[151] Ibid, v.14.
[152] NCV, Matthew 17: 20.
[153] Ibid, 21; 21.
[154] Ibid, 17: 17.
[155] Ibid, 21: 21.
[156] 1 Corinthians 13: 2.

you ask me for anything in my name, I will do it."[157] The ability to "do greater" and "ask me" only fuels the idea anything can be done. Greater accomplishments easily can refer to greater larger effects with wider implications. Whatever is great, it will be greater. Besides, the ability to do "all things" has to be only in comparison to what previously could not be accomplished. So let us get real about asking Jesus help to do anything. However, no need to rule out the possibility for unique miraculous events. It is wise not to be presumptuous about God, because it is not possible to know God's next line of action.

17

Perfection! It does not mean flawless nor sinless. Perfection means to be complete. To be Christian that is complete, even though pieces of their abilities of personality are not fully actualized, is possible. The Christian's new identity from their new self collaborates with the incomplete personality to fulfill realized abilities of personality. We know there's more to us than how we live. This is parsing with the meaning of perfection. However, that is exactly how God looks upon everyone's possibilities, especially the Christian. The Christian ought to get it: they already are on their *becoming* encounter and collaboration between the old self is dying off, as the new self grows into what God has intended. God sees the potential becoming an actual. The Christian also has the possibility to see themselves as God does, for what they can be.

18

For the Christian, an archetypal shift of perspective has altered their view of God and reality and of themselves. The Christian sees themselves as perfect or complete, in respect that their incompleteness no longer infers life is falling apart, unhinged. Rather life is falling

---

[157] NCV John 14: 12, 14.

together as they understand Christian spirituality and God, and that intimates cohesion and identity with the new sense of self. This is Christian spirituality.

19

Jesus mentions what it means to be complete/incomplete as an intimation of perfection, for those who want to believe in God. First, we need to be perfect, and, to be perfect as God is, takes the idea to another level. We could flare a defensive snappy comeback that glares with heat, to tell Jesus, "Either do it yourself or get lost." The presumption is not one of us is perfect, as a human person, in respect that mistakes are made with the wrong word or committing the wrong deed. We sin! Jesus, however, did just that, told us we can be perfect as God is perfect. Let us unpack that.

Jesus is in the zone on a lengthy talk instructing how to live a righteous life. Then approximately midway through, as if the righteous living was not enough, he injects a by the way line, a short line in no uncertain terms, "So you must be perfect, just as your Father in heaven is perfect."[158] Is it possible to be perfect "just as" our Father God? Context is called for, if only to even out the odds, which is an unfair comparison. To be perfect "just as" sounds like a challenge. The short answer, to be perfect like God means to be complete in spite of mistakes. We should not presume God never thinks he has made mistakes[159] initiated by human freedom. To

---

[158] NCV, Matthew 5: 48. Compare James 1: 4; 3: 2, perfection is completion as to "have everything you need" and, in spite of "mistakes," and "if" (ESV) not for perfection, "control" (NCV) of the body would not be possible, inferring that it is possible.

[159] Genesis 6: 6, 7; 1 Samuel 15: 11; 1 Chronicles 21: 15; Jonah 3: 9, 10. Usually such examples indicate God changed his mind, had a better attitude. However, that does not mean a mistake has not occurred. God changed his mind, but to claim God had no regret because of a mistake is intellectual dishonesty, as if to say God's regret is not identical to human regret; we're made in his image, therefore it is identical.

be perfect, according to Jesus signifies to be complete, since God is complete. To be perfect is to be complete, having reached some sort of product, finished off better than before. Therefore, to be complete has to include our reason for being, the purpose or function towards an aimed for end. Such an end, always is attached with a person's calling, their summoned to a way of life or mission and/or a way of vocation; usually both. God knew what he is all about; so does the complete person. The complete person understands their full nature.

A person finds, either by accident or deliberation, they detect their calling as their place in the world with the purpose of completion. The other side, to be perfect or complete is, to borrow from Paul and attach it to what Jesus has taught, "Christ love is greater than anyone can ever know, but I pray that you will know that love. Then you can be filled with the fullness of God."[160] "So you must be perfect, just as your Father in heaven is perfect."[161] Put together, these verses crackle with deep insight to be perfect is to be filled up, as God is full. It puts a new take on the phrase, "They are full of themselves." Anyway, a Believer knows, what the love from Jesus is like, only then is there presented the opportunity to go deeper, to "be filled with the fullness of God." The word power tool "fullness" means to be full to the top, in all of, which something is, thus is complete. So, what does that fullness look like? This fullness leads us back to what God is like (short list). The parawords for fullness are descriptive: love, guilt free, not falling to pieces, refusing to be insecure, satisfied spiritually, and being reasonable and wise – this is perfection as completion.

Moreover, Jesus explains that the style of water he gives for spiritual sustenance, that person "will never be thirsty." [162] The word "never" always explains itself: as if without end, to ever continue, never cease from effect. That is identical to the fullness connection that excites spiritual longings to be satisfied, with a full complete satisfied

---

[160] NCV, Ephesians 3: 19.
[161] Matthew 5: 48.
[162] John 4: 14a. See, 6: 35.

soul. Negatively speaking, Paul speaking to the Ephesians (verse 19), his expectation for these Christians, they will eventually experience "the fullness of God," although it slightly infers that perhaps not all Believers have such an experience. Nonetheless, how does a Believer know that they have arrived perfectly and completely in the fullness of God? The answer gets very close to what Jesus said about not being thirsty again. What does it mean to not be spiritually thirsty? The best pick for answer is *satisfaction*. To be as God is to be satisfied is to be free, from the power of sin, just like God.

20

Maturity has an impression, it impresses, leaves its imprint upon those that are immature to emulate; has the feel of maturing, gradation and stages, with phases so that a comparison is made of previous conditions of maturity. The mature gradually ascent, grow and move from one condition of being to another condition of being – spiritually and intellectually, which translates existentially and philosophically. Within each of these stages of maturation there is completeness, there is satisfaction. This maturity presumes growth is continual or frequently occurs with some regularity; not continuous as if without a break, nor without a plateau spiritual experience of feeling stalled.

21

Personality and identity show off character, or, shows up character for what it can become. This signifies that God is working with the Christian to grow deeper spiritually and to advance intellectually. Therefore, each stage of growth can be measured, quantified, and compliments previous stages of gradation. Christians can look back on events past, and be a witness to their own evidences of maturation and completeness.

22

There is no need for self-righteousness, which is a close friend of perfectionism; it is antithetical to Christian spirituality. Moreover, the perfectionist is constantly nitpicking standards and values to death because they are never satisfied.

23

Occupational life requires the imputation of meaning, because work by itself is without meaning to feed the soul, the internal reality of the presence of the self.

24

When it concerns work, the job we do for a living requires the impute of soul. It is soul work for deeper significance, on the job training. This is soul work on the job and through the job. Significance on the job reveals a calling to do the job, however immediate or long term. Our calling as a vocation with meaning forces us onto inquiry as to why we do what we do. Is it only for the money? Alternatively, is it prestige, status? Should there be at least one altruistic drive in what we do for a living? Does every job afford the luxury to give it deeper meaning? In a similar manner, we need to ask what various characteristics of our personality are doing for us – on the job. It may require imagination, but how we answer these questions and inquiries, is likely to give any job a higher calling and purpose.

25

Deeper meaning will cause any job done and imputed with a higher calling and a transcendent purpose will please God and ourselves. The job done well with a deeper meaning gives work and gives self-esteem, the encouragement for a job done well. If that is not possible, then perchance, we are in the wrong job.

26

Employer and employee Believers are advised about the conduct of work. The Believer is not to be rebellious and belligerent as an employee. The Believer as an employer is to regard their employee with dignity. The biblical reference concerning employer and employee conduct has the unfortunate use of dated language, to differentiate these two groups as slaves and masters. Putting that aside, the principle is easily dragged out. Paul encourages these two groups of Believers, that as Believers they belong to each other. He tells them both "Do your work with enthusiasm. Work as if you were serving the Lord, not as if you were serving only men and women. Remember that the Lord will give a reward to everyone, slave or free, for doing good."[163] The critical point here is that the job can be accomplished with less pressure when it is done "as if" they were "serving the Lord" so then the Lord can "give a reward" over and above what payment is rendered for doing the expected. The proper competition for a job done, rewards will be given either immediately or in the future life or both. Either way, when the job is completed as if for the Lord, there is an extra attachment, amendment to the payment. How this will be distributed is not delineated. It further stipulates that work should be done "just as you obey Christ"[164] and "do this not only while they watch you, to please them"[165] but "do what God wants as people who are obeying Christ."[166] In other words, if you are an employer or employee, do the right thing for what you are paid. However, do not do the job to kissyface and be subservient.

We should rather bring to the workplace, from our awareness,

---

[163] Ephesians 6: 8.
[164] Ibid, v.5.
[165] Ibid, v.6.
[166] Ibid, v.6.

that our *new self is a difference making a difference.* We impute deeper meaning into the job, into the performance of work itself is a confirmation of our calling; transcends doing it just for the money. Likewise, doing the job as only a vocation but lacks proper reimbursement however enjoyable seems a bit short sighted. Financial compensation while doing what we love to do,[167] is a blessing from God.

27

Significance – meaning, to signify as to indicate or point this out from that other – is a paraword that deals with, confronts the smug sarcasm often associated with what is socially acceptable apathy and indifference. Significance, therefore, has its crosshairs aimed at the bloated self-importance of political correctness. It is easy to locate; simply follow its stench to insignificance.

28

Diagnostic questions probe, deal with, our nothingness when we focus on our sense of self and our place in the world. Ask yourself questions: Have I become too comfortable, indifferent, towards the contradictions and tensions attached to my life? Has caution and anxiety held me back, caused vulnerability to overpower? What prevents me from experiencing deeper depths of meaning? Why do I feel incomplete no matter what efforts are accomplished, and is that bad or wrong? Do I think too much in one-dimensional terms, lacking imagination? Such philosophic diagnostic questions point towards significant directions. The main cause for self-esteem is when an accomplishment is achieved, and that achievement is considered significant.

---

[167] Proverbs 12: 14; 16: 3; Ecclesiastes 2: 24, "eat, drink, enjoy their work. . .comes from God."

29

James Hillman crackles with the obvious as he puts it, "An education in any way neglects imagination is an *education into pathology*. It is an education that results in a sociopathic society of manipulations. We learn how to deal with others and become a society of dealers."[168] James Hillman has a catchy play of words. He has done, turns "dealers" from a negative drug infested death wish, turning it into a healing withdrawal, detoxification from *wanting* sociopathy. We just do more than cope; instead, we deal with problems by attending to situations. To deal with is to work with word power tools. To deal with, also, means to attend like a shepherd, to what needs attention, not run in the opposite direction. Giving up is absurd.

30

Paul an apostle has a short pithy line that packs a punch. Short sentences often have that character. Paul encourages Believers, "Try to learn what pleases the Lord."[169] The *English Standard Version* has "discern" for "learn." Since these Believers are enlightened, as the previous verses state, Paul reminds them that Christian spirituality isn't all about getting the right ideas stuffed into the head, insofar, such ideas should correctly trickle down into the heart or soul – they are to at least attempt to try to please the Lord. Ethics and worthy behavior reaches the heart or soul. Inasmuch, this "try to learn" is a self-referential term by pleasing God there is an actual practical experience of satisfaction to be a learner as a Christian. The Christian then goes out in the world where ideas and practice are tangled with reality. To tangle with reality means the possibility to entangle due to difficult situations that show off the character of the Christian. When

---

[168] *City & Soul*, p.92.
[169] NCV, Ephesians 5: 10.

reality is dealt with, character is on display, there is achievement, and a perfectly completed condition of being that pleases the Lord.

31

Discernment is the critical feature of Christian spirituality to help to catch on to attend what is important. Discernment is with wisdom, to ascertain deeper truth about God and the brand new self, juxtaposed from the attention grubbing old self. Discernment reveals a connection and disconnection in the soul, not that presence of the self with its definitions and pieces of identity are falling apart – but the process of falling together – as we become. Pieces, like fences, need mending. Soul work is soul-making, which works towards the finished reasons for being a someone. The soul work to be a someone could never be achieved as an actuality, without the work of the Spirit of God, and wise discernment to ascertain deeper truths.

32

Sure enough, the soul, the internal reality, the presence of ourselves, has an intrinsic need to know. The soul has the need to grow therefore. Otherwise, the soul is in perpetual incompleteness, never arriving with some completeness or perfection, full or inflated, which only occurs until there is connection with God. Sometimes it is as simple as that; other times it seems more complex, complicated. Don't ever worry about it.

33

Instead of dealing with the push and pull of our existential trek and spiritual journey, a sojourn (an old turn of a word), a short visit, has the desire for the deeper spiritual life. According to Alan Jones, who writes, [W]e seek short cuts to life everlasting."[170] The search

---

[170] *Journey Into Christ*, p.58.

and journey that is sought, however, that excludes God, happens when people are jumping all over the place, from one eventful experience after another. Jones continues, "One short cut is by way of experience. This is an age in which people are understandably desperate for experience. Experience is just as dangerous as the web which is woven around the mystery. Experience can be a drug, which, in the end, destroys or obscures the very reality that gives rise to the experience. We stagger from experience to experience: each time needing a larger shot of it than last."[171] There is bungee jumping, well, there also is experience jumping. Experience jumping is jumping from one spiritual fast food seminar event, only to dine on experience, and nothing more than flighty events to another, ad nauseam. There is no difference with people who jump from one endless vacation experience to another sunny hot spot experience. They are restless, not knowing how to be. Tidbits of insight and wisdom packaged as quick-fix jeweled trinkets – never satisfy. In another book, Jones throws out a justified complaint, "Today experience is more highly valued than beliefs, so we should begin with experience. But this has its dangers, partly because experience does not exist on its own. It needs some filter to help us understand what we've experienced. Few realize that they rely on unexamined beliefs to interpret what happens to them. They just know that they have a hole in the soul. They feel lost. Some of them feel like losers."[172] You know he is right.

"When it comes to Jesus," explains Jones, "we begin with finding ways to experience his presence. It's tricky because experience is an odd thing. It's a hybrid – something caught between an event and its interpretation."[173] What is supercharged is the experience is going to occur. How we manage, the experience depends if we manage it before it manages us. Relying upon experience alone is by itself not enough to satisfy. The use of words as power tools to help ground

---

[171] Ibid, p.58.
[172] *Reimagining Christianity*, p.46, 47.
[173] Ibid, p.194.

the experience imparts some quieter intelligence. Meanwhile, Jones admits, "In short, if we start with experience (and I think we should), we're in for a rough ride. We're wedded to poetry, myth, metaphor, and the dangers of subjectivity. That's why we need each other to keep testing reality. We make Jesus in our own image."[174] Experiential knowledge as there is with respect to salvation does not preclude easy smooth glide into consistent spiritual harmony. We ought to expect a "rough ride" sometimes, because we are dealing with the leftovers of our old self.

34

Spirituality grows with its slowly revealing insights are seeds that by their own necessity or structure are a slow-grow spirituality, often imperceptible until noticed later, by inspection of previous behavior patterns of thought. Consciousness catches up with what the unconscious already understands. That is how we know that we know since a truth has already been recognized. Spiritual growth is not imagined therefore.

35

Of course the Christian gets it, that God has been shepherding all along their spiritual sojourn. Did you believe the Christian arrived alone in their sojourn? The Spirit of God produces the results for spiritual growth, in spite of all the intellectual curiosity of study. The Spirit's job is to produce fruits of the Spirit, whereas the Christian longings become satisfied through faith in the process. The results of this spiritual sojourn are human qualities (fruits) produced by the Spirit.

---

[174] Ibid, p.194

36

God sees the unnoticed potential in the process of becoming an actuality – in us.

37

In spiritual growth, the new finally becomes old, just another level of gradation, and nuanced levels of completion – although nothing in that growth becomes insignificant. There has to be an acquired taste for humility in spiritual growth. The perception is, that more is yet to be experienced. Otherwise, there is an indulgent perfectionistic perception of personal development. It is a myopic view that there is always something else that must immediately be overcome. It is an insult, a hubris perfectionism to Christian spirituality not to have humility, especially because of growth involves time-released spiritual advancements.

38

Christian spirituality that does not have a philosophical bite to it, nurtures a Machiavellian sociopathic troublesome mindset, or, a narcissistic political correctness gristmill grinding out groupthink that is spiritual pulp fiction. A philosophical bite denotes the skill to bite off, prune the excesses of love that fosters useless ideas to hang on the vine of spirituality, only to get in the way of spiritual maturity. To bite off is to prune is to cogitate, insofar, not to bite off more than the philosophic can chew.

Be Someone, It Takes Faith, Trouble, Temptation

1

Some people with a slight Kierkegaardian slur turn "that individual" into a negative. The contemporary minds of such people do not want individual people to think for themselves. Rather, they want the collective we, to grubbily snarl and riot for groupthink. It takes faith to believe in yourself, which means to think for yourself.

2

The Bible is not concerned about our precious feelings in the least. It often speaks in terms that are emphatic, either do this or be that – not too much of the wussy prefatory stuff like "perhaps" or "probably" are not used as power tools; for what we should be or do. The Bible comes right out to encourage someone that can stand out to live what they believe. To include a prefatory caution: to be a *someone* is to stand out from being a *somebody* like every other somebody that amounts to a nobody. It takes faith to be a someone instead of somebody who is only like everybody else. A someone is more than a mere somebody like every other somebody. Another prefatory caution: make sure the soul is anchored securely. As it is noted, we need not be like some: "Continue to have faith and do what is right. Some people have rejected this, and their faith has been shipwrecked."[175]

3

The Christian that has a fear of God, especially when they do wrong or say something stupid and hurtful, does lack understanding about their relationship with God. Apologies may be in order to someone else, but the Christian's disposition has a safe healthy fearlessness. Faith rivets tight. The Christian should always be willing to be thankful for God's forgiveness however. Mulling over sins and the need for forgiveness is a futile exercise because the Christian who is mulling, that is a direct negativity on how life is lived. Anyway, the Christian already is forgiven for past, present, and future sins. Acknowledge and accept the forgiveness, then freely move forward in life.

4

To be appreciated by God for believing he exists and for giving forgiveness of sins is a freeing experience from the negativity of guilt because there is a connection between the experience of salvation and the practice of being guilt free into an expression that the Believer as a person is intermingling peacefully with other people. The result of faith in God, because of Jesus, has the freedom to be, to be a someone.

5

Faith has a need. It does not matter how strong, nor the amount, of faith – however strong and amount could represent. The quality of faith cannot cover up faith's required need, regardless of who a person is, as if, each of us could contribute to meet the need faith

---

[175] NCV, 1 Timothy 1: 19.

has. The need faith has is to become "pure" or to be "tested" so that its "genuineness" will become evident.

From Peter an apostle, he records that troubles are to be reconstituted, reconsidered for one greater aim. The objective that faith be improved: "Through these troubles come to prove that your faith is pure. This purity of faith is worth more than gold, which can be proven to be pure by fire but will ruin. But the purity of your faith will bring you praise and glory and honor when Jesus Christ is shown to you."[176] The *English Standard Version* reads to conclude the "tested genuineness of your faith" which is "precious" although it can become vulnerable and "perishes though it is tested" but the advantage is it "may be found to result" in a favoured status with Jesus. Regardless of what version is read, faith needs to become more effective by external "troubles" (verse 6), by the hard knocks of life and existential angst.

At first glance of Peter's critique on faith gives the impression faith "can be proved to be pure by fire," as though that were a onetime event. Useless weight of dross, caked on waste, which creates impurities, will be burned off. How often, rather, does our faith need its impurities burned off? How often may depend upon the ineffectiveness of faith. The impurities that cause faith to be ineffective are anything that is considered strong enough to ruin it.

6

Nowhere does the Bible infer or outright state that faith is given by God, particularly for salvation. Faith belongs to each person, neither supplied on piggyback from friends or relatives or family experience. Faith is, or it is not, as it is individually experienced. Faith has an *isness* quality to it, anyhow, functions ineffectively or effectively.

---

[176] NCV, 1 Peter 1: 7.

7

To be outstanding as a someone signifies to have faith in the effect of the salvation event to draw out deeper abilities within personality. The process that draws out abilities is a crucial aspect of sanctification or growing spiritually as evidenced by improved personality and character. What is pushed or pulled in growing, to the surface of personality and character, is an identity to identify as one's own.

8

What is right anchors itself in what is righteous. This is what Old English identifies as *rihtwis*, understood as *rightwise*. Therefore, that which is "right" signifies what is "wise" demonstrates itself as "rightwise" or "righteous." The word "rightwise" is a lost word today. I'd like to see it return to common usage, perhaps as a paraword to be attached as a helper for wider understanding about being righteous and being wise simultaneously.

9

From our earlier introduction to Peter, he is often portrayed as impetuous, a bit of a blockhead, compared to Paul. Peter does not appear as an intellectual giant. Revisionists deconstruct to suggest that perhaps Peter could not have written his letters; I really do not care. Paul may have dictated some of his letters and gets a pass from critics, whereas former fisherman Peter does not. Letters by Peter, meanwhile, demonstrate how much he advanced spiritually and intellectually. From an average somebody as a person, Peter became a someone as a person. So, when Peter speaks, we should listen. What Peter has to say, should be added as a spiritual rider, amendment, to what Paul has to say about the fruits[177] of the Spirit

---

[177] Galatians 5: 22-25; perhaps Ephesians 5: 7-20.

and the armor[178] of God, of both, the Christian should have as part of their nature or to be put on as part of their character. Specifically, what Peter teaches the Christian, "you can share in God's nature, and the world will not ruin you,"[179] because, he delineates characteristics added to their identity. Such characteristics make it possible to live an effective life as a someone. Nowhere else in Scripture does it teach about sharing in God's nature. Inasmuch, Peter was ahead of other thinkers and movers of ideas, or he is off, way over his head. He was ahead, not over his head, because to share in the nature of God suggests intimate relationship.

10

Peter's list of paraword power tools that can be attached to our identity help us be a someone, because as Believers, we "share in God's nature."[180] A someone is not just a nobody as a mere somebody, but is a Believer to whom God "has given us everything we need to live and serve God."[181] The words Peter rattles off are attached to our identity, used metaphorically, like a ratchet wrench that snaps on a particular sized socket, picked from other sockets in the set. Each socket is specific to do a particular sized job. After all, such a tool is not called a "ratchet socket set" for no good reason. Peter's list as parawords function as a ratchet socket set. Indeed, such words are not the "everything" Peter said God gives. His use of "everything" would include anything that works to the advantage of spiritual maturation.

The paraword list to help us toward maturity is: faith attached to goodness; that to knowledge; that to self-control; that to patience; that to service to God; that to kindness; that to love. The results are to be "useful and productive in your knowledge of our Lord Jesus

---

[178] Ephesians 6: 11-19.
[179] NCV, 2 Peter 1: 4. Context, verses 3-11 lists characteristics as a spiritual rider.
[180] NCV, 2 Peter 1: 4.
[181] Ibid, v.3.

Christ"[182] However, the results of not adding such characteristics is to "not see clearly" to such an extent that a Believer "is blind and has forgotten that he was made clean from past sins"[183] although if such tools are used they "will never fall."[184]

11

How can someone forget that God has made them clean, cleaned them up spiritually? How can they forget where they came from? Become absent minded is normal at times but not always excusable, however, with Alzheimer's disease, some forgetfulness is tolerated since it is a *dis*-ease. Selective amnesia, just being a cultural Christian, has no excuses to forget the price Jesus paid for the offer of salvation and sanctification. Otherwise, living the Christian life can become so normal and natural that intellectual laziness or nearsightedness sets in and the unexamined life becomes natural, leading towards the ineffective life. It is a sad and pathetic commentary. Such willful forgetfulness further suggests some people forgot the Socratic maxim: "The unexamined life is not worth living."

12

Paul, prefaces with what he wants to say, that the "spiritual person is able to judge all things." Paul is attracted to something Isaiah has said. Paul tells us while quoting Isaiah who posited, "Who has known the mind of the Lord or been able to give him advice?" What Paul really wants to say as he shoots back an answer to his strawman question, as if blazing with both barrels: "But we have the mind of Christ."[185] With

---

[182] Ibid, v.8, context 3-11, v.8. ESV renders this, "ineffective or unfruitful" which seems more convincing.

[183] Ibid, v.9.

[184] Ibid, v.10.

[185] NCV, 1 Corinthians 2: 15, verse 16 quotes Isaiah 40: 13 about "who knows the mind of the Lord . . . to teach him?" Paul uses "teach" but Isaiah has "advice."

such a short but loud sentence, this is a shot heard around the world; a game changer, a sensational "sea-change" to borrow Shakespeare. All the same, Paul has the audacity to answer an old question. With that line, Christians got it: they can have the identical perspectives that God has. Paul did not consider that mindset for perspectives too difficult. Christian spirituality – sometimes even God himself had troubles dealing with worldly problems – is not as difficult as some presume with perspective.

13

Characteristics for becoming a someone is a guilt free pure clean conscience. Therefore, not living life limited by a bad conscience. The guilt free clean conscience has a rightwiseness mindset. The person can understand through the practice of living a life of faith, signifies being set free from the power of their old self, however, they can only have such a mindset because the perspective is viewing themselves as a whole from the new self. Comparisons are made with their old self. Their conscience provides a guilt free clean sense of themselves. A guilt free, not neurotic, conscience is wiped clean. That is not a one-time event, rather is continuous as a condition of being as a new self.

14

Today we have the popular handed down phrase, first penned in 1637 by René Descartes, "I think, therefore I am." Frederick Copleston has an interesting paraphrase of that Descartes line, since Descartes is dealing with doubt and epistemology. Copleston puts it as, "However much doubt, I must exist: otherwise I could not doubt."[186] That is bang on right. Descartes meant the "I" is a clear distinction from the physical body; classic pure dualism. I have no difficulty with dualism, of soul and physical body co-existing. The non-purest dualism is

---

[186] *A History Of Philosophy*, p.90, vol.4.

125

closer to reality, that the soul has a close connection to the body, as if both were one yet holding two properties or styles that complement each other. After all, when the body dies, as it goes, so too does the soul leave the body. Furthermore, accounts from Christian records, as opposed to Greek reaching back to Babylonian antiquity, Christians did not accept the view of the immortality of the soul. Rather, Christians to present time accept the view that the soul is given immortality[187] since it is dead to God, or numbed senseless. The soul's need is to be alive with the added feature of eternal life. However, this is going off slightly in another area. For the spiritually minded, dualism skirts around the immortality of the soul.

As Descartes is read today, for some, it is now turned on its head, into what was never intended. Some claim, "I am therefore I think because I feel it." This claim says in effect, that the "I' is the material physical body only because they feel it, which introduces a singularity as if what is felt is the real "I" and could not be otherwise. Such a view makes biology destiny, which then nullifies the feelings of the "I" creating a nonsense conclusion. Besides, thoughts are not feelings.

15

A Christian, who understands what they are all about as a someone, will attempt to think what God thinks to be important. They want to know how God appreciates the realities of the world he created. Understanding those interests gives an idea about who God is. As Paul informs us about a dark mindset, that God disproves since "people did not think it was important to have a true knowledge of God. So God left them and allowed them to have their own worthless thinking and do things they should not do."[188] "In the Lord's name, I tell you this. Do not continue living like those who do not believe. Their thoughts

---

[187] 1 Corinthians 15: 22, 53, 54. Compare John 3: 14-16; 6: 27; 12: 50; Galatians 6: 7, 8; 1 Timothy 1: 16; 2 Timothy 1: 10.

[188] NCV, Romans 1: 28, context, verses 17-32.

are worth nothing. They do not understand, and they refuse to listen. So they cannot have the life that God gives."[189] It is possible either as a pseudo-Christian or a Christian of a kind (cultural Christian), to have some faith, but live from what their material body restricts them to or allows them; anything goes. Alternatively, some aver, Paul refers to nonbelievers, who may have believed however now do not. As Paul says, "They knew God, but they did not give glory to God or thank him. Their thinking became useless. Their foolish [senseless] minds were filled with darkness."[190] The clincher is verse 28. They did not live by faith, but rather the desires of the body with some aberrant ideas or methods of thinking, particularly regarding sexual conduct. Succinctly, Hedonistic: think it, just do it, in a negative sense. As Paul reminds the Ephesians, "not to continue living like those who do not believe." Such people "invent ways of doing evil" and "applaud others who do them."[191] Indeed, that kind of mindset is easy to acquire when people do not "have a true knowledge of God."

What is pinned down, thinking becomes worthless, senseless, it lacks quality and reason's power. God then decides to leave such people to their own demise. Next, feelings are confused for thinking. Making decisions on feelings as thoughts for personal definitions, even sexual identity, is too dubious, fickle, since feelings can change on a whim. Rather, to become an authentic someone is to trust the sanctification process of growing spiritually by "working to complete your salvation" but do it "with fear and trembling, because God is working in you to help you want to do and able to do what pleases him."[192] What opens the dark mindset is first; there is no "true knowledge of God"[193] but simply a few nobodies that are just a few somebodies who are

---

[189] NCV, Ephesians 4: 17, 18.
[190] NCV, Romans 1: 21. I'm unconvinced as to who these people are, either Christian of a kind or nonbelievers of a kind. I suspect Believers at one time, but not now. The way they think, is deceptive.
[191] Ibid, vs.31, 32.
[192] NCV, Philippians 2: 12b-13.
[193] NCV, Romans 1: 28.

self-righteous where anybody can choose not to be rightwise. It is the opposite of "God working in you" kind of mindset. The question for us: Can the authentically serious Christian have a dark mindset? That is a crucial dark question Some insist ought not to be asked because it opens contradictions, which suggests dark answers. How much light of insight is allowed into any answer, probably, depends upon the level of mature advancement been achieved from the old self to the new self.

16

The Christian keeps in mind word power tools provided by Paul, such as the "Spirit of God" as the "Spirit of Christ" acknowledged as the "Spirit of Jesus Christ."[194] Attach those word power tools to the concept that God does a good job working with their personality, the Christian has evidence that God is working with their life and their faith is effective. Affirmatively, such ideas complement our emotional condition of being. Thoughts and feelings fit in with the personality, meaning there is no split. It fascinates how anyone can volunteer to toss that away! That act has all the marks of philosophical suicide.

17

Unlike sin as defined by missing the mark, the standard, whereas evil is all about hitting the target. The essence of evil is destruction, by covert sociopathic malevolence either with strings attached or by outright hostility and hate. Evil seeks to destroy. Hate and violence seeks what is an evil intent.

18

The Christian who is caught in a psychic bind, perhaps not exactly the wrong thing, but must decide for the right thing, is stuck in a dark

---

[194] NCV, Romans 8: 9; Philippians 1: 19, respectively.

place. For years, what has worked effectively with positive results can begin to work against, in spite of good intentions. The bind becomes sticky; fixation on why it is happening causes anxious times, become obsessive, insecure, and neurotic, disordered, not relaxed, useless speculations only enhance guesswork into whether that is all there is. Identities get lost, undefined, or difficult to express authentically. Perspective is more than lost, it has been tossed, settling by muddling around in the sticky middle, thereby, becoming mediocre. These times when old ideas worked effectively, suddenly, do not often occur during middle age. It only becomes a crisis when perspective is tossed. Midlife crisis is for the uninformed. The end is near wild card thinking – only if the Christian forgets how to use their word power tools and trust in God for wisdom. Wisdom takes note that the situation is only a possible crisis in the making. The end is not near.

19

Mediocrity kills soul work. Mediocrity is weird. It has that comfortable familiarity with a tagalong expectation that nothing lasts, therefore, after a while it becomes nauseously tolerable; like being in a cul-de-sac. A cure from the condition of mediocrity is a skeptical doubt that questions everything, instead of a corrosive cynical doubt that weakens faith and diminishes authenticity and personal authority. If we're not careful, full of care for soul-making, authenticity, personal authority, and a skeptic's doubt will be killed and mediocrity settles in.

20

Paul Tillich writes, "The courage to be is the courage to affirm one's own reasonable nature over against what is accidental in us."[195] He later clarifies that, "Not conformity but differentiation is the end of

---

[195] *The Courage To Be*, p.13.

the ways of God. Self-affirmation of one's uniqueness and acceptance of the demands of one's individual nature are the right courage to be."[196] He assures such an affirmation, "This does not necessarily mean willfulness and irrationality, because the uniqueness of one's individuality lies in its creative possibilities."[197] As Tillich explains, "It is not justification of one's accidental individuality. It is not the Existential courage to be one's oneself."[198] The courage to be one's new self has the confidence to accept acceptance as a functioning term for the participation in the justification by faith. Acceptance causes the sense of being justified by God, as a present condition of the reality of God's grace. That is the experience as the courage to be a someone. Tillich says, "The courage to be in this respect is the courage to accept forgiveness of sins, not as an abstract assertion but as the fundamental experience in the encounter with God."[199] The acceptance as justification by God, literally gives a guilt free clean pure conscience. Christians are assured "So now, those who are in Christ Jesus are not judged guilty."[200] The courage to be signifies the courage not to be guilty, in personal "reasonable nature." Especially, free from the corrosive guilt from a neurotic sensation, for what we are not responsible. Neurotic guilt is feeling guilty for what we did not do. The "reasonable nature" is our human nature that consists of natural freedom to move between the will to do bad (sin as self-centered, against God) or to do good (please God, care for another); except now in the new self, given through salvation, has the courage to be free from guilt regardless of how we may feel.[201]

---

[196] Ibid, p.117.
[197] Ibid, p.117.
[198] Ibid, p.165.
[199] Ibid, p.165.
[200] Romans 8: 1.
[201] Compare 1 John 3: 20, 21.

21

On the subject of God's grace, ordinarily as God's love, has a connection to estrangement or sin. Paul Tillich notes, "Grace, as the infusion of love, is the power which overcomes estrangement. . . .The first mark of estrangement – unbelief – includes un-love. Sin is a matter of relation to God and not to ecclesiastical, moral, or social authorities."[202] Tillich continues, "The doctrine of the universality of estrangement does not make man's consciousness of guilt unreal; but it does liberate him from the unrealistic assumption that every moment has the undetermined freedom to decide in whatever way he choose – for good or bad, for God or against him."[203] Grace does remove the burden of the consciousness of guilt. Insofar, "There is only 'The Sin,' the turning-away from God, and from 'The Grace,' or reunion with God. These are qualitative and absolute, not quantitative and relative, categories. Sin is estrangement; grace is reconciliation."[204]

However, turning to less theological (?) source, Tillich denotes grace: "Do we know what it means to be struck by Grace? It does *not* mean that we suddenly believe that God exists, or that Jesus is the Saviour, or that the Bible contains the truth. To believe that something *is*, is almost contrary to the meaning of grace. Furthermore, grace does not mean simply we are making progress in our moral self-control, in our fight against special faults, in our relationships to men [people] and society. Moral progress may be a fruit of grace; it is not grace itself, and it can prevent us from receiving grace. For there is too often a graceless acceptance of the Christian doctrines and a graceless battle against the structures of evil in our personalities. Such a graceless relation to God may lead us by necessity either to arrogance or to despair. It would be better to refuse God and the Christ and the Bible then to accept Them without grace. For if we accept without grace, we do so in a state of

---

[202] *Systematic Theology*, vol.2, p.49.
[203] Ibid, vol.2, p.57.
[204] Ibid, vol.2, p.57.

separation, and can only succeed in deepening the separation."[205] Such acceptance is only an intellectual acknowledgement, a polite nod, and grace never changes the spiritual condition of being. Participation in salvation thus excludes experience. Accordingly, such are those who are nothing but cultural Christians.

We could push Tillich's premise further. The "graceless" produces a poor ineffective malfunctioning worn out power tool, repetitively, doing "battle against the structures of evil in our personalities" to no good results; always needing another fix, another personality repair through therapy, because there is a split between our old self and our new self; both can still be noticed. The idea is that less of the old self, rules personal life. Not to have the new self as the influence, intimates less spiritual growth. The possibilities of sanctification is the work of the Spirit of God, so that, our new self by spiritual regeneration, renewal and reconciliation, has more than overcome the old self, but its old power to influence, holds no attraction for who we are as a person in Jesus.

22

Jockeying for quick access is the ubiquitous sneaky power of temptation. Temptation has power, but no authority. Temptation is an empty suit. Nevertheless, it is not toothless. When it bites, you'll know. There is an old catchphrase "temptation and tribulation" or "trials and temptations." Either way, those two either are not identical or function independently, yet in a sneaky way, where the one is, the other follows.

23

It appears, if faith is mentioned, often the subject of temptation, is not far behind. Anyone who desires to be a someone, which is

---

[205] *The Shacking Of The Foundations*, p.161.

to be authentic with substance and character, must contend with temptation. Someone that identifies with their identity as their own precious self, will overcome and deal with temptation as paramount concern. Discovery of an opposing otherness revels personal strengths. Someone that does not have a sense of self cannot deal with temptation, will not acknowledge its power; mercilessly coping that temptation need not be reckoned with, or it will go away. Likewise, temptation is not necessarily evil, although it competes for interests. For sure, too often, when temptation is mentioned, evil is not far behind.

24

From James an apostle, we have an insightful critique: "When people are tempted and still continue strong, they should be happy. After they have proved their faith, God will reward them with life forever. God promised this to all those who love him. When people are tempted, they should not say, 'God is tempting me.' Evil cannot tempt God, and God himself does not tempt anyone. People are tempted when their own evil desire leads them away and traps them. This desire leads to sin, and then the sin grows and brings death."[206] God is not porous to allow evil to flow through his nature and be fooled by evil. Since God, then, understands that the power of temptation can bring ruin, he does not tempt his Believers; they can do that enough on their own. The function of temptation is like a hunter who hunts, sections off, and corners for the kill. Anyone familiar with an unrelenting, even if covert, temptation understands how it feels as though one is hunted and cornered. Except, usually, temptation *brings* a self-inflicted wound(s) that strikes deep into the soul only for an immediate gratification. To remove the cornered feeling, all that has to be done is create physical space and convince that yielding is not necessary. Temptation has the sense of immediacy to it; it must

---

[206] NCV, James 1: 12-15.

be done now, can't wait. Such an inordinate irregular, either natural or unnatural, although supposedly a harmless desire, leads all the way to evil, which leads all the way to spiritual death. The hunt for the kill of the soul, may take time, but sins often are revealed. Some presume the wounded soul fairs better when temptation does not lead to destruction. However, the wounded soul has psychic injuries that go deep to cripple true satisfaction.

The style of temptation literally is exclusively to cause a stumbling reaction, to inflict a wound of a scandalous sin. Temptation hunts for the opposite of what we know should be done. When there is no opposite, then there is no temptation. Knowing the difference makes sin less attractive. However true that is, for the spiritually mature, temptation is utilized as a tool, designed to work for them, not against them. That is the freedom of Christian spirituality and the power to resist otherness with God's grace; provides spiritual strength and confidence. Shifting the emphasis away from the hunt of temptation (the attraction), flips the power of temptation back onto itself, effectively nullifies its power. That shift and nullification is accomplished to embrace the complications (accept their realities) due to temptation as a reality to be faced. Temptation is looked at head on. There's no need to yield to it. We learn from the experience of being hunted, what to avoid and expect. This removes the power of temptation for the glitter of attraction has lost its luster, significance. Character teaches what they are made of. Temptation confirms it. Therefore, as James says the Believer is "tempted and still continue strong, they should be happy." That takes faith, confidence, spiritual strength, and rightwiseness, to arrive on the other side of temptation.

Standing tall to resist temptation, however, can become trickier, because the spiritual person is not fooled as they were before. Temptation can become complicated, crafty, with complex what-if scenarios, weaving a tangled web of philosophical rejections, insecurities, innovative destructive ideas, only to develop a complex. Walter Scott accurately penned the familiar line in 1808, "Oh, what a tangled web we weave/When first we practice to deceive."[207] However, there is more to temptation than playing the trickster. Jesus was led by the Spirit into the desert;[208] God utilized temptation and the devil as his tool. We rather shrug the event off, assured Jesus could handle it; which he did and told the devil, Satan, where to go. Furthermore, Jesus teaches us about prayer, says this odd but fascinating line, of what is known as the Lord's Prayer, "And lead us not into temptation, but deliver us from evil."[209] Believer is to ask God not to lead them into temptation, as Jesus knows too well, that is what his Father did to him. The intimation is that God is in charge enough to lead, but not in control of every unimportant detail, since evil can run amuck of things. If we must ask God not to allow us to be tempted, suggests there is more freedom we have at disposal. God, rather, does not have control of everything, but is in charge to rescue us from existential troubles. The Believer learns to have a relaxed wise caution through the growing process.

25

Meaning and significance do not arrive on their own. Meaning and significance arrive in our lives either by God or by chance, by temptation and tribulation. The hard knocks of life with God's grace, we learn wisdom to discern, to become a difference making a difference.

---

[207] *Marmion*, stanza, XVII, citation from "allpoetry.com," anonymously submitted.
[208] NCV, Matthew 4: 1.
[209] ESV, Ibid, 6: 13. The NCV has toned down voice: "And do not cause us to be tempted, but save us from the Evil One."

THIS THING CALLED FAITH

1

The intimate and friendly relationship with God is a sojourn for Christian spirituality that has a style of spirituality immersed in what is a tight faith. This tight faith means to have faith in the spirituality presented, as it is experienced, through the Spirit of Christianity. The result is a unique offer of peace that is satisfaction. That faith in the spirituality presented trusts the growth of its spirituality, and trusts that God is ultimately concerned for the Christian's future condition however immediate or distant. A tight faith trusts in faith for a trust in God, namely because of Jesus as the Savior. Faith rivets tight.

2

Here are some biblical references what faith is like, what it looks like in ordinary practice, then some clarification. Each reference if from the *New Century Version*, and some words are in added italics. The list of verses for attention about faith is: 1) "The Good News [salvation] shows how God makes people right [righteous] with himself – that it *begins and ends with faith*. As the Scripture says, 'But those who are right with God will live by faith.'"[210] 2) "So now, *those who are in Christ Jesus are not judged guilty* [no condemnation]. Through Christ Jesus the law of the Spirit that brings life *made me free* from the law

---

[210] Romans 1: 17.

137

that brings sin and death."[211] 3) "The Lord is the Spirit, and where the Spirit of the Lord is, there *is freedom*."[212] 4) "Now I am right [righteous] with God, not because I follow the law, but because *I believe in Christ*. God *uses my faith* to make me right with him." "I do *not mean that I am already as God wants me to be*. I have not yet reached that goal, but I continue *trying to reach it* and to *make it mine*."[213] 5) "How much more is done by the blood [life] of Christ. He offered himself through the eternal Spirit as perfect sacrifice to God. His blood will make our *conscience pure* from useless acts so we may serve the living God." "And since we have a great priest [Jesus] over God's house, let us come near to God with a sincere heart and a *sure faith*, because we have been *made free from a guilty conscience*, and our bodies have been washed with pure water."[214] 6) "These troubles come to prove that *your faith is pure*. This *purity of faith is worth more than gold*, which can be *proven by fire but will ruin*. But the purity of *your faith will bring you praise and glory and honor* when Jesus Christ is shown to you."[215]

Next, clarifications about the details of faith. From the start, faith obviously is what a person has, therefore it cannot be a characteristic, quality, or style belonging to anyone else – it belongs only to that particular person. Therefore, affecting salvation, it *"begins and ends with faith"* potentially for the wannabe Believer, however specifies in actuality for all Believers *"those who are in Christ Jesus are not judged guilty"* because they are *"made free"* from what works against their nature. Faith, therefore, allows personal experience to know *"freedom"* on how God exists is in a condition of *"freedom."* None of this freedom to be, and, none of this freedom from guilt, can ever be possible without the predicated sacrifice from Jesus of his life and death and resurrection. Once the decision is made to believe in Jesus

---

[211] Ibid, 8: 1, 2.

[212] 2 Corinthians 3: 17.

[213] Philippians 3: 9b, 12.

[214] Hebrews 9: 14; 10: 21, 22.

[215] 1 Peter 1: 7.

by faith to admit, "*I believe in Christ,*" then God "*uses my faith*" and the estrangement, odd disconnect between God and the Believer is absolutely removed. Meanwhile, there is more "*not mean that I am already as God wants me to be*" the Believer can assuredly claim they are "*trying to reach it* and to *make it mine.*"

This is evidence of the work from the Spirit of God to acquire a "*conscience pure*" free from psychic junk. This conscience made pure gives affirmation the Believer has a "*sure faith*" having been "*made free from a guilty conscience.*" After all the spiritual growth and intellectual astuteness obtained throughout a lifetime in relation with God, the Believer has caught on, "*your faith is pure*" and the "*purity of faith is worth more than gold*" even though "*proven by fire but will ruin*" if not made strong and effective. The result is worth it since, "*your faith will bring you praise and glory and honor*" as recognition from Jesus Christ for a job well done. Faith is, or it is not, as it is individually experienced.

Moreover, this is far from the detested Pelagian premise that suggests those who choose to believe and use their faith, somehow, have contributed to the content and method of salvation. Therefore, the Believer can freely decide with Paul, as a practice of faith, "Since we have been made right with God by our faith, we have peace with God. This happens through our Lord Jesus Christ, who has brought us into that blessing of God's grace that we now enjoy. And we are happy because of the hope we have of sharing God's glory."[216] That is not bad faith, what may as well be unfaith, rather faith that is impure, weak and ineffective, effeminate and needy, soft in the middle. Impure faith is brittle, since not tested by temptation, produces brittle spirituality. Authentic faith, Paul tells us, is claimed, owned, and practiced in a real dirty world. Faith has the audacity to look at any adversary in the eye, stare down an opposing otherness, and works with word power tools as parawords to deal with problems that need fixing, knowing time and the future is on its side. Faith outlasts.

---

[216] NCV, Romans 5: 1, 2.

3

Real, authentic faith cooperates with God. There is cooperation because nothing can be contributed to salvation, redemption and justification. This faith is alive and crackles with rightwiseness. It hits the road running, where the rubber hits the road, and is versatile, flexible, to be practiced outside of the head and into the real world. Real faith and the real world belong together. Authentic faith has a relaxed wise caution, trusts God, but has an eye open for what is essential to divide the truth from the other "stuff."

4

If faith, is given by God for salvation, then God can take it away. If faith is given as a gift, when, by arbitrary and capricious self-indulgence, makes God into a despot, fickle and biased to favor others at the expense of the other schmucks. It must be understood: I do not believe there is such a God, nor would I desire such a God. Does it require an insecure faith to believe in that kind of God and blind, unquestioning belief? It would for me.

5

The Christian cannot participate in the new self unless there is faith. The new self needs faith to be itself. The bottom line, faith must cooperate with God for the effect of the work of the Spirit of God.

6

Some Christians mistaken faith as a gift from God. The source of this mistaken label is in the famous reference from a misreading of Paul's words. He says, "I mean that you have been saved by grace through believing. You did not save yourself; it was a gift from God.

It was not the result of your efforts, so you cannot brag about it."[217] The phrase "I mean" harks back to verses 1 to 7, particularly they were "spiritually dead because of sin and the things they did against God." Somebody can be dead spiritually but that does not signify they do not have simple faith. The phrase "it was a gift" is a direct line of fire to its source of grammatical aim: "been saved." The word "it" does not refer to faith. To insist "it" is about faith, instead of salvation, forces an interpretation that does not carry the concept or the grammatical aim. Any forced interpretation must be suspect as an attempt to falsify a concept; it is intellectual dishonesty, at worst, intellectual bigotry or narrow thinking using thinking for a nefarious purpose. Faith is never a gift; cannot be given, either by God or by anyone else – not for salvation.

7

Questions about faith for those who believe it is a gift: What does it mean to receive faith as a gift, what is involved in that giving so that the person understands they have it? How would they know that faith was given or if they already had faith? By handing out faith, does God give tiny pieces of his own faith, or is it created and then given? Does God have faith in the person who believes? Is faith borrowed, on loan, temporary? Does God view faith as a commodity that can be discarded or die, have an expiration date? That question is not odd, since no faith will be required in heaven – supposedly. According to Jesus, faith is often depicted as small in a negative way.[218] Should the Christian, if God gives faith, expect quality faith? Why is faith impure, low grade, ineffective, needs to become pure? Moreover, if God is handing out faith, why is every Christian's faith different, either large or small? If faith is given so that one Christian receives more than another, is God prejudiced with indifference?

---

[217] NCV, Ephesians 2: 8, 9.
[218] Compare Matthew 6: 30; 8: 26; 14: 31; 16: 8: 17: 20 for a short list.

Moreover, why is it, no Bible reference can answer these questions in the affirmative? Because faith is not a gift from God for salvation, and principally for anything else.

8

Those that claim faith is a gift from God, misunderstand that they express a philosophical concept, not a theological premise. The thinking is unintelligible because they presume to speak theological when it is philosophical. Such twisted pretzel theology-philosophy is contradictory to our reasonable nature as a freedom. It is contradictory because humans, made after the freedom of the nature of God as his likeness – pretzel ideas are simply wrongheaded ideas. Therefore, wrongheaded ideas are unintelligible with its disturbing hubris and philosophical mistake. The philosophical mistake is the presumption it is theological, which conceals a hidden belief that each Believer, particularly, is chosen by God. Such thinking is conjecture, guesswork, and promotes bad faith, which is ineffective; promotes brittle spirituality riddled with insecurity. Such faith, that is required for such perspectives comes more from the intellect, from the head as a good place to begin however, although lacks some life to reach the heart. Faith must reach our "reasonable nature" as Paul Tillich[219] calls it. This sleight of hand or dexterity of mind mistakenly accepts a philosophy for theology that is filled with hubris. It opens the thinking process to the possibility for influence by the demonic. Only destruction is derived from such arrogant ambitious inordinate pride. Most Christians will naturally wince, if they consider faith as a gift, that they could be open to the demonic. The demonic, after all, seeks to use the unreasonable, the unintelligible, even the simple mindset to be agreeably open for wrong-headed ideas. Run from it! Wisdom is not unreasonable.

---

[219] *The Courage To Be*, p. 13.

9

Jesus gives an interesting story[220] about the gospel message and the use of intelligence with faith. Someone is planting seeds. Inadvertently seeds fall on rocky soil and ground with more weeds than is appreciated. Birds also eat some of the seeds. Some soil is good enough to grow a crop, while other seeds died. All the same, some seeds took deep root and others did not. That short rendition hopefully doesn't do injustice to the story. The "ground" as metaphor is not to be overextended to infer a redeeming quality about people; Jesus did not consider that a possibility, since that is not the point of the story.

The explanation of the story Jesus supplies is, random falling seeds are like people that did "not understand" the message, and then some sort of "Evil One comes and takes it away."[221] Meanwhile others understand enough to "accept it with joy"[222] in excitement and enthusiasm, however, they do not "let the teaching go deep" to affect their personality and character, down into the soul, only to, "quickly gives it up"[223] therefore. Still, for others that also chose to believe, in spite of it, "lets worries about this life and the temptation of wealth stop that teaching from growing."[224] This last group functions in reverse: instead of running to God for help, they go the opposite direction. The flight mode of operation as reaction has the ability to "stop that teaching" and stop it "from growing." The maxim is, we stand still to grow roots, to become as God intended. To become deep rooted with substance, is a sort of seriousness for that which matters. Any of us, at any time, are as deep as our roots have gone.

Insofar, Jesus says the seeds with roots produced fruits, results

---

[220] Matthew 13: 3-23.
[221] Ibid, v.19.
[222] Ibid, v.20.
[223] Ibid, v.21.
[224] Ibid, v.22.

and advantages, because such a "person hears the teaching and understands it" often at various times, and "sometimes a hundred times more, and sometimes sixty times more, and sometimes thirty times more."[225] Such people listen to positive ideas, and then they catch on, only to produce beneficial advantages for their self-worth and spiritual depth. The difference that catches attention of Jesus is that some people try to understand deeper meanings, literally making the examined life worth living, for soul-making. Indeed, we are convinced to be convicted to be converted. Seeds of truth that are planted in the soul produce knowledge of the process involved for growth and faith it will happen.

10

The writer of Hebrews pins it for *the classic* definition for faith, without a drop of a word that it is a gift from God or anyone else. Stating clearly, "Faith means being sure of the things we hope for and knowing that something is real even if we do not see it."[226] Authentic faith intimates, not being blind, but is "being sure" so the "knowing that something is real" is not about a faith walking in the agnostic dark. Spiritual illumination causes faith to be a practice, a way of being. Such a practice is experienced while dealing with and believing, what can be seen and the unseen. Limiting faith only to what "we do not see" diminishes the insight on how life can be lived with certainty. Anything else as a wise perspective for faith is just a dream and possibly bad faith. Bad faith is nothing more than a blind faith; takes leaps without forethought. It is not a stretch of the imagination to aver, however, faith that is unquestionably alive, has the confidence to laugh at the agnostic mindset of mental gymnastics with an insecure antipathy for a conclusion. There is nothing wrong arriving at a point where conclusions can be lived with and reasonably

---

[225] Ibid, v.23.
[226] NCV, Hebrews 11: 1.

acceptable assumption have the weight of authenticity. However, to have an abhorrent dislike for conclusions seems a bit odd and insecure and a lack of faith for the process of deduction perhaps more than the data deduced.

CLOSE HERE: TOWARDS A FUTURE

1

What the Christian has is a future, and, a style attached to their spiritual experiences that functions with their idiosyncratic personality traits. This deals with the new self as opposed to the old self predicated upon the salvation event working with the sanctification process of spiritual growth with its intellectual astuteness. The effect is a new philosophical frame of reference, without exception, looks forward with an improved future practiced and led by Jesus the Shepherd. Eternal life begins in the here and now. Then again, for now, there is a place of rest, a peace that is satisfaction.

2

Faith and Rest. "We who have believed are able to enter and have God's rest."[227] Those words cut to the point by its writer, that not every Believer may enter into a deeper level of spirituality, since that is the point of the "rest." A few sentences before, it sets up that suggestion, "Now, since God has left us the promise that we may enter his rest, let us be very careful so none of you [Believers] will fail to enter."[228] This reminds us of what Jesus said, there are those "who hears the teaching and quickly accepts it with joy. But he does not let the teaching go

---

[227] Hebrews 4: 3a.
[228] Ibid, v.1.

deep,"[229] therefore unable to experience God's rest, which refers to a spiritual condition of being, or, a way of the condition of being. This rest is a place to settle down to be still and enjoy relief, ease and comfort, by being relaxed with a wise caution, because God is just a prayer away. The spiritual rest that God offers does not have fear. The rest that is given by God has a peace attached to it, sort of when something comes together and it makes sense: Peace is satisfaction.

Inasmuch, spiritual rest is getting away, by using faith, from the annoying dull burden associated with the old unredeemed aspect of human nature. Relief from the dull burden of trying to be good or trying to be sinless is removed. We may sin less, certifiably, but never sinless. The burden of trying too much to be good, even the attempt to be good just enough, finally, is removed and useless guilt becomes powerless to cripple personality. This is by entering God's rest by faith. We cannot work our way into that resting place. This peace is from God is a gift. The Believer as a Christian becomes at ease with God, for the relationship functions as a friendship, not estranged or dysfunctional. Additionally, such a spiritual rest teaches that we give in, to God, as God through Jesus gives us, so we do not have the need to give up. This giving in without giving up is definitive faith.

3

Use of Freedom, Kick Guilt to the Curb. The mature Christian, without exception, can know what they are all about – not determined by feelings, but how God reacts to, and deals with, their idiosyncratic personality as a person who has the courage to be, to be what God has intended for them to become. However, the power of sin and the misuse of freedom which is the freedom denoted as human nature, often prevents that process of becoming, into an actuality; namely by

---

[229] NCV, Matthew 13: 20b, 21a. Compare, Matthew 11: 28, 29, Jesus says to accept him is to have "rest," relief from psychological "heavy loads" associated with the hard knocks of life, and no philosophical conclusions that can be lived with.

feelings instead of biblical ideas, standards and values, that does not work against themselves nor other people.

Guilt intimidates and freezes the use of freedom to be unfree. We then, talk what we should accomplish or talk ourselves out of ideas. Alternatively, guilt is like an acid eating away substance and significance, meaning and depth of our "reasonable nature" (Tillich). Then, our reasonable nature becomes unreasonable. We can only do this by freely using our freedom against our authentic better self-interests. As Peter Koestenbaum succinctly puts it, "Nothing automatic is authentic."[230] To be authentic, or, not to be authentic, that is the question. Each of us must freely decide on how to use our freedom to deal with personal concerns. Authenticity encourages to melt the cold freeze often felt that encloses guilt, that can only occur by using the freedom of our nature. The reason nature of our human nature works with the power from God to set us free, free from feelings of insignificance and a shallow existence. For the Christian, guilt becomes mostly useless because it can freely be ignored, that's right, ignored if it needs to be ignored. Likewise, the Christian has the freedom to not feel guilty about not wanting to be guilty. Freely kick guilt to the curb. There needs to be a deliberate contemptuous attitude towards guilt, in order to freely be authentic. Koestenbaum is right; it takes effort to be authentic, since it will never happen on its own.

John an apostle, pins what the philosophical perspective describes, "This is the way we know that we belong to the way of truth. When our hearts make us feel guilty, we can still have peace before God. God is greater than our hearts and he knows everything. My dear friends, if our hearts do not make us feel guilty, we can come without fear into God's presence."[231] The intellectual takeout is that God is greater than our secretive internal reality or soul. Therefore, God knows everything that is going on in there; nothing

---

[230] *The New Image of the Person*, p.135.
[231] NCV, 1 John 3: 19-21.

hidden in our hearts God is able to hunt it out, for the Christian, that is a comfort not despair or anxiety. This verse indicates that God knows everything there is to know, although debateable, it is annexed as a consoling reassurance that God is in control or in charge. The additional feature, however, when there is no excessive criticism and self-condemnation, we will naturally be more confident to be in "God's presence" with no fear whatsoever.

4

No Survivor's Guilt. The Christian philosophical perspective is to have a new frame of reference, disposition, especially about not being guilty and not feeling guilty for not feeling guilty. Since God has forgiven every possible sin, either performed, or will perform, carry into effect (we are performers of our sins), the frame of reference has a grasp of the larger picture of putting guilt in its proper place. Guilt, often, has its gaze internal, therefore tends toward myopia, blind to the good, the sinless. This alludes to what is in the New Testament: "The Good News was preached to us just as it was to them. But the teaching they heard did not help them, because they heard it but did not accept it with faith."[232] It takes faith to accept and not be blind to what is believed that God removes the burden of guilt. That is not merely a belief. It transcends believing to accept as clear as day. Moreover, to hang on excessively to guilt when not necessary, as a Christian, is to insult God for making it possible to remove the guilt of sin. The reality of such a frame of reference is that it creates a new mindset that fits effectively with the new self due to the new spiritual second birth. The Christian who has "accepted it with faith" lives their whole life in freedom.

Of course, the all too familiar maxim from Paul makes sense for a new frame of reference regarding the consequence that guilt has lost its destructive effect: "There is therefore now no condemnation

---

[232] NCV, Hebrews 4: 2.

150

for those who are in Christ Jesus."[233] Guilt, insofar, ought to be felt for doing something wrong. Rather, neurotic guilt which is guilt as a condition of being, since the Christian is "in Christ Jesus" its condemnation mode of operation is nullified. Jesus claims the spiritually blind, are blended to, or soaked in guilt, so close to it they are unaware of guilt. Jesus says, "If you were blind, you would not be guilty of sin. But since you keep saying you see, your guilt remains."[234] Jesus is telling religious pedantic types with a bit of sarcasm, which they assume to see, to grasp the insight of deeper spiritual interests, but they do not. It is as though Jesus says, "Oh yeah, by the way, you are so unbelievably clued out, you are as guilty as sin, mostly because you claim to see. I don't buy any of it." They have smoke in the mind's eye. The Christian should be free from the grip of useless guilt, and then the smoke clears so they can have better insight into their spiritual sojourn.

Because the Christian is to be growing spiritually, and because they should not have any survivor's guilt, their spiritual sojourn holds on for a rough ride at times. They deal with temporary contradictions, tensions, psychic hurts, cuts to the soul, purification of their faith, philosophical disappointments about their identity, assured therefore, "God began doing a good work in you, and I am sure he will continue it until it is finished when Jesus Christ comes again."[235] Furthermore, they can know what that finished look will be like. It says that "your love will grow more and more. . .have knowledge and understanding with your love; that you will see [catch on] the difference between good and bad and will choose the good. . .be pure without wrong . . .filled with the good things produced in your life by Christ to bring glory and praise to God."[236] The Christian becomes God's artisanship – his

---

[233] ESV, Romans 8: 1. The NCV has "not judged guilty." Compare Romans 1: 17, to live by faith.

[234] NCV, John 9: 41, context, 35-41. Compare Matthew 15: 14, stay away from the spiritually blind.

[235] NCV, Philippians 1: 6.

[236] Ibid, vs.9-11. Compare Ephesians 3: 19.

personal make-work project – so that what works for that Christian will not work against them or others. God sees us all as an unfinished work in progress. Except God has a good idea what the finished look will be like. From the creation story, God created what he made. "God looked at everything he had made, and it was very good."[237] Speculation whether God was thoroughly pleased with his handy work or a bit surprised how good it looked; probably both. Since God has confidence that he can do a "good" job at creating, the Christian can trust God to finish[238] the work he began in their spiritual soul-making. God can see that work and be pleased. The finished look for the Christian will see the light of day, just as God's creation, to be free from neurotic guilt. However, this freedom does not give the right to be a psychotic sociopath or the local insecure bully and involved in criminal activity. The Christian is to try to some extent, to get along with people, without a pinch of guilt. Some people, without surprises, cannot be pleased, while others are not worth the effort. There is no advantage feeling guilt for ignoring such people.

5

The Future Begins. When a person gives their life to Jesus, a new future begins. An intense stare commences towards the future rather than too much looking backwards. The mindset is: that was then; this is now with a nudge forward. This frame of reference, the Christian can notice their progress of spiritual growth, which is not a fast, but a slow-grow, spiritual and intellectual advancements. The entire idea of *becoming* has the notion of the slow-grow, time released experiences in personality development and in relationship with God that is future oriented without losing sight or connection with the present. Using the creation story as a metaphor, even God completed creating, he moved on to other interests. The past is always a part of who we are,

---

[237] NCV, Genesis 1: 31a. compare verses 10, 12, 18, 21, 25, everything is "good."
[238] Philippians 1: 6.

but the Christian cannot be constantly looking over the shoulder to what was.

Consider what Jesus states about sacrifice involved to follow him, which is only recorded by Luke: "No one who . . . looks back is fit for the kingdom of God."[239] The idea is whoever has their gaze attached, longingly, wide-eyed, to what is behind them, and is not ready for use, properly placed or matched for spiritual interests. If attraction is still for the former condition of being, then they are not a fit because their attraction is not forward looking. Something that is a slow-grow and time released must be present to take roots and acquire worthwhile stability, while attention is for forward advantages in spiritual growth. In this way, the future does not turn out to be unbecoming. To become, is to come about, hence the use of the phrase, which authenticity is to know what someone is all about. Besides, Christian spirituality may feel at home with trench warfare, dealing with evil and otherness, but as it is in any fight, the eye is on the future, on what is ahead.

Oddly enough, the word "future" is not used much throughout the Bible. The Bible has scant talk or dances around futurity, like not having a future. Paul mentions that, "All things belong to you" for our spiritual benefit, not to exclude "the future."[240] Then later to Timothy, Paul informs that the Believer is able to build a "strong foundation for the future."[241] However, with an intimation of futurity, a writer in the New Testament assures "you will surely get what you hope for . . . [like] those who through faith and patience will receive what God promised."[242] Hope is not a consideration. The future works with "faith and patience" for which the future would not outlast the present. We learn to stand out from the old self, into the new self, with its stare towards the future. Sometimes two steps forward with

---

[239] ESV, Luke 9: 62. Compare Ecclesiastes 7: 10, not wise to claim "former days better."

[240] NCV, 1 Corinthians 3: 22, 23.

[241] NCV, 1 Timothy 6: 19. Compare Proverbs 24: 13, 14.

[242] NCV, Hebrews 6: 11b, 12b.

a misstep of one step backwards, although living with the future in mind. Christian spirituality is future oriented, however immediate.

As Peter Koestenbaum aptly puts it, "To have a sense of the distant future is to have meaning and hope. To have a sense of the mediate future – the future that mediates the present with the distant future – is to have connected present activities with future results."[243] That is wisdom with discernment. This means not to have difficulty to accept the future, to look at it, as it seems to come toward us. Further, he says that because there is a conscious connection with reality and freedom with "a sense of unity and continuity" provides for "The person feels that the present is connected with – and is unfolding of – the past, and that the future is the direct consequence of how in the present he uses the material from his past. This person learns from experience and has a sense of his own future."[244] The future is more of a pull than the past pushing us along. Maybe it is not always important to know our past but build upon what we already understand. The past sometimes – too frequent – holds us back. The salvation experience provides a fresh start for a future that is definitely worth it.

6

Carving A Character. The word "character" indicates either an instrument or tool for making marks, borrowed from *Latin* and Greek, like a chisel or it means the distinctive nature of that which is carved. Character is made, can be changed, carved, unlike personality that seems to be there as a constant familiarity at the foundation, from the beginning of personal existence. Character is made, altered and changed. Character is responsive to social conditions and to the impute of good ideas. In effect, character is thereby cut into shape. The carving of character from the "stuff" we are made of – personality

---

[243] *The New Image of the Person*, p.352.
[244] Ibid, p.403.

idiosyncratic traits that are a constant familiarity, social conditions and word association with ideas – our historical past hints toward future actualities. Shaped and carved into a better character is soul work, with a future to present a personality with presence of soul. Carving character is soul-making. Soul-making is God "doing a good work" "on working to complete your salvation"[245] for the purpose of an immediate future and a distant future.

Working in the background of soul-making, especially for the Christian seeking authenticity and authority for personal effective living, is God's persuasive and benevolent enlightenment nudging along "to help you want to do to be" so that they are "able to do what pleases him [God]."[246] Such a carving process is not a laissez-faire, laid back, indifference to what God is doing for us. Carving involves participating in the learning process about that which matters, being interested, paying attention, tooling around with parawords, listening to the longing of our internal reality the soul. Like the stone carver who chisels at the marble to carve out a character, which allows its presence to be revealed, so does God carve our character into its shape by bring out deeper and better aspects of personality with an identity identified as our own. God takes from our past and what we are made of, and reconstitutes that into something worthwhile. By what is cut away from the parts that work against the personality, we discover a new identity to identify as our character. The is the new self because of salvation.

7

Temptation Is A Wisdom Tool. Here is a repeat[247] of segments specified: "Temptation has power, but no authority." "Someone that

---

[245] NCV, Philippians 1: 6; 2: 12.

[246] Ibid, 2: 13.

[247] Temptation is mentioned in "Be Someone, It Takes Faith, Trouble, Temptation" particularly in sections 22, 23, 24. The selected quotes here are respective of these numbers.

does not have a sense of self cannot deal with temptation, will not acknowledge its power; mercilessly coping that temptation need not be reckoned with, or it will go away." "Temptation hunts for the opposite of what we know should be done. When there is no opposite, then there is no temptation. Knowing the difference makes sin less attractive." "However, there is more to temptation than playing the trickster. Jesus was led by the Spirit into the desert;[248] God utilized temptation and the devil as his tool. We rather shrug the event off, assured Jesus could handle it; which he did and told the devil, Satan, where to go. Furthermore, Jesus teaches us about prayer, says this odd but fascinating line, of what is known as the Lord's Prayer, 'And lead us not into temptation, but deliver us from evil.'[249] Believer is to ask God not to lead them into temptation, as Jesus knows too well, that is what his Father did to him." As temptation becomes trickier, we become wiser. We must become accustomed to the use of wisdom as a paraword power tool. It is wise to turn temptation into a paraword force that does not work against self-worth or security. Using the power of temptation against itself, also is a tool, which confirms our dexterity with word power tools and we know experientially where the line is; how far to go without being burnt, deceived, taken for a long ride nowhere.

Paul Tillich asks pointedly the obvious about temptation: "Under what conditions is temptation serious? Is not one of the conditions an actual desire toward that which has the power to tempt? But if there is such desire, is there not estrangement prior to the decision to succumb or not to succumb to temptation? There is no doubt that under the conditions of existence this is a human situation."[250] An inappropriate desire, if yielded to, is the only desire that can become a sin. Desire by itself does not lead to inappropriate acts or to what is a sin. Therefore, something intrinsic about the desired object or even,

---

[248] NCV, Matthew 4: 1.

[249] ESV, Ibid, 6: 13. The NCV has toned down voice: "And do not cause us to be tempted, but save us from the Evil One."

[250] *Systematic Theology*, vol.2, p.128.

excites towards temptation. If nothing attracts, then to be tempted fizzles out the desire. Even though the imaginary image is still present, what is tempting may still burn with an amber. Therefore, imagination excites the desire, and when it is inappropriate and yielded to, sin and troubles arise to compound life's heavy lifting. Jesus[251] told us he wants to help to remove the heavy burdens, including those we bring upon ourselves. Incidentally, why would angels be tempted, while in the presence of the Lord God? Simply put: the will to power. Possibly the will to power to control the attraction is the power to sin. In the future, some day, life will be lived with no propensity to sin. Now, that seems like theory. But, is it? When temptation is not yielded to, is there not a hint of what it will be like not to be tempted?

The biblical writers natter on about spiritual battles[252] but do not supply enough wisdom on how to fight the good fight. The Christian is not encouraged to look for a knockout fight, indeed not, with temptation or the devil or anything that has the potential to destroy. Temptation, often, is easy to find without effort to hunt for it. The mature Christian rather understands, usually from experience (dealing with, tooling with it), what is their limitations, and know when to back off. In addition, they have caught on to get over themselves, and acquire some humility and realism about what they are all about. Temptation is about narcissism: I deserve better. I deserve more. As Paul instructs, "Do not think you are better than you are. You must decide what you really are by the amount of faith God has given you."[253] This is faith for a specific purpose: proper evaluation of our own self. A wise realism regarding ourselves has the wisdom grounded in faith that has a proper evaluation, with respect to how much equivalent temptation can be dealt with and not be overpowered – given for a particular task. As Jesus succinctly pushes the idea, "But wisdom is proved to be right by what it does."[254] Those

---

[251] Matthew 11: 28.

[252] 2 Corinthians 10: 3-5; 1 Timothy 6: 12.

[253] NCV, Romans 12: 3b.

[254] NCV, Luke 7: 35. Compare Ephesians 3: 10 intimates layers in wisdom.

who possess her by the results evidenced in personal life, they know wisdom.[255]

The point is wisdom enough to know our limitations and not tempt fate. The fact that temptation is present, anyhow, means we must deal with it, by resisting temptation we gain practical insight into our limitations, where the line is not to be crossed. The other option goes beyond avoidance of temptation, but deny it is present. The New Testament writers warn, regardless that the devil is an enemy looking for anyone to destroy, they also claim, "Refuse to give in to him, by standing strong in your faith."[256] By simply "standing strong" or standing tall, we demonstrate how fearless we can be. "So give yourselves completely to God. Stand against the devil, and the devil will run from you."[257] It is an odd mixture: resistance equals running. The devil may see more in us than we often recognize in ourselves: God, authority, wisdom. Wisdom discerns and experience confirms that which is a temptation for one person may not be a temptation to another.

To resist temptation may require intelligence, although it certainly demands spiritual strength to "stand strong." Not every intelligent person knows how to use intelligence, however. Wisdom is discernment for the insight demanded for the rightwise action. Wisdom is there if we want it, otherwise she will let us go loose. The old Greeks, for the love of wisdom, wisdom is *Sophia*, and is therefore feminine in power, thereby proven right by her results. Wisdom is found in what captures our interest, to what we pay attention to. Attention is given to temptation. However, temptation is not utilized by loving it. Love is never enough. Because temptation is an opposing otherness, it will roll over love only to distort lust for love. Love brakes down. However, love is a common denominator and often a first reaction for Christians. Love levels out. Love can be tapped out,

---

[255] Proverbs 24: 13, 14, as honey is sweet and good, so "wisdom is pleasing" with a "future."

[256] NCV, 1 Peter 5: 8, 9.

[257] NCV, James 4: 7.

no more to give. Therefore, a paraword tool such as resistance has a greater effect to have the dexterity to deal with temptation.

8

This Thing Called Love. That caption, it reminds of the song by *Queen*, "Crazy Little Thing Called Love." Anyway, a different perspective about love from Jesus. Jesus rather commands that Believers love each other. Act with love and the feelings will follow. He speaks clear enough, "Love each other. You must love each other as I have loved you."[258] Love as a command has carved markings into character however. Love is the premise from which behavior stems. Jesus goes on, "All people will know that you are my followers if you love each other."[259] What would Christians be like if love was not a principled feature? History demonstrates schisms, and taking people to court.[260]

Love, evidentially, is blind. It is an art of wisdom to overlook someone's mistakes or a character defects. However, it is not wise to be convinced that is what Jesus had in mind. The person shown love, patience, and forgiveness also has the responsibility to reciprocate love and understanding. Otherwise, the unteachable person shown love is a hard nut to crack. The Christian perspective of love is very much at home with wisdom and discernment. Therefore, wisely executes correct action towards the unteachable.

What crackles through the veins of Christian spirituality is what its writers insist. They insisted the extended long reach of the law of love. Love demonstrated by Jesus is that love from God obligates the Christian to catch on to "know that love" which ultimately is also "Christ's love."[261] Such a love develops a "purified" internal reality

---

[258] NCV, John 13: 23.

[259] Ibid, v.34.

[260] 1 Corinthians 6: 1-6, Christians went to court to solve problems with those who were known to be Christians.

[261] NCV, Ephesians 3: 19

or soul cradled in "true love"[262] especially for fellow Christians. Christians "should love each other" since their "love comes from God," therefore, each Christian "knows God" and that is how they identify "God is love."[263] This does not infer that any love is from God; however, what permeates the Christian community of fellow sojourners as Believers. Recall Christians terrorized in various sections in the world. Do we have love for them? Do we feel for them? Is there love or some overlooking to the social outcast within our local Christian community? Is the contradiction of such people in isolation, inevitable? Such contradictions are an existential disturbing reality, which perhaps has been throughout history since the inception of Christianity to welcome the philosophical outcast. Comfort is cut off at the head by todays terrorist. The love as an integral aspect of Christian spirituality, notwithstanding, for its characteristic style to be interested, cradled in wisdom and discernment, freedom and free from guilt, relaxing in a clean pure conscience, sharing in God's nature and rest, while *living* in the actuality of a new self with a new consciousness.

9

A Needful Style. Acquiring our own sense of style is more of a discovery than a methodical plow through self-help books, or academic studies in philosophy and psychology, or any humanities course. That is the point. Style is close to what interests us. We pay attention with interest. Is curiosity the handmaiden to wisdom? Wisdom cannot be attained without curiosity. Wisdom loses its cutting edge of discernment, and is high in the sky, useless and impractical. Wisdom gives direction, although curiosity assists to give it the aim that discernment provides. Within such characteristics of personality is the discovery of style. Style, however, is more subjective and personal,

---

262 NCV, 1 Peter 1: 22.
263 NCV, 1 John 4: 7.

possibly individualistic and distinctly unique to any given person. Each one of us is one of a kind.

Friedrich Nietzsche, say what you want about him, but he does come out with some gems of insight. Nietzsche's claim is, *"One thing is needful. – To 'give style' to one's character – a great and rare art!* It is practiced by those who survey all the strengths and weaknesses of their nature and then fit them into an artistic plan until every one of them appears as art and reason and even weakness delight the eye."[264] It is "needful" Nietzsche tells us in his usual outstanding style, to give "style" to "character." Christian spirituality provides an opportunity to develop a style of our own that is needful to express our spirituality, not as an inordinate out of character style, but in character with personality, showing itself off as a worthwhile person of substance. Such a style developed through the process of spiritual experiences has a depth to know how to think and live accordingly. That means it first pleases the Lord then the person doing the living accordingly. However, with a kindred Hippocrates style not to intentionally attempt to harm.

10

Ballast Effect With Style. The ballast effect is to have sense of balance between the personality and spirituality, which is the process of soul-making. The effect of the ballast seems more prevalent during the growing stages when spiritual process of sanctification is more prominent, as opposed when growth seems less evident. Sanctification is where aspects of the personal begin to fit with the character and identity of the Christian. They become more authentic and empowered with a sense of belonging, often with the discovery of their calling or purpose in life. Style is a paraword to assist for the ballast effect between spirituality and intellectuality, between

---

[264] *The Gay Science*, p.232. For those unfamiliar, the English title initially was "The Joyful Wisdom" but its original has stuck.

the personal identity definition of personality and the spiritual aspect of the internal reality of who we are, as evidential in character and what we do with life. When the balance between spirituality and intellectuality is lost or not considered important, there is disconnection of the person and the external world. Spirituality becomes airy, flighty, and intellectuality becomes sloppy and sluggish, watered down, flying too high. Icarus is falling.

The ballast metaphor is helpful. There is a ballast in electrical systems, plumbing, ships; the crushed stones that enclose railway ties are a ballast – all with effect. The ballast is to control, regulate, and balance off excess power or water flow, to keep railway ties in place. The ballast keeps us placed, even keeled, prevents wild tangents with respect to how we grow spiritually and intellectually. Where the soul is deflated there is imbalance, out of place. The ballast allows for a constant ebb and flow of the free exchange of ideas. This inflates the soul with insights we can choose any positive words as parawords, for they are power tools attached to the ballast effect. Words such as soul work, soul-making, relaxed wise caution, perseverance, stability, give in without the need to give up, wisdom, authenticity, authority, becoming, – is a short list to work with.

Working with parawords for good ballast effect, style takes such word meanings to integrate with Christian spirituality. Style, therefore, avoids the threat of too much conformity to groupthink, abhors indifference that makes it impossible to make a difference. Style satisfies the endless search, both for personal and career, life. The ballast that does not function, allows to flow of tangents in endless searches for ephemeral exercises: Jumping from one event to another event. Or, doing the lazy way by moving the arrow on the computer monitor while you stare at a screen like a voyeur of other Christian's in worship, or another sermon and lecture; spirituality via virtual reality ad nauseam. The ballast is an impartial tool; use it with care and wisdom, and style will not work against the soul work that is longed for. The ballast is the internal sense, an awareness and realization of the obvious; perception, illumined by education and by hard knocks of life. The ballast effect works extremely efficient with wisdom and discernment. Like any ballast, it senses too much or too little.

The ballast effect with style helps to prevent excessive literalism, which is aberrant fundamentalism. It also prevents the intelligibility functioning between spirituality and intellectuality, causing the spiritual life to become dry or stale. Frequently, such a condition of being is not a spiritual problem but a philosophical difficulty about spirituality. If the spiritual life becomes dry or stale, it is due to being bored with excessive routine or literalism. Mystery is demystified. Answers to questions are presumed to be consumed, believing no more pesky questions with nuanced answers. These people are the bored again. The ballast effect has attention paid to soul-making, which is healing. Otherwise, personality is broken, neurotically incomplete. Healing of the soul using parawords, working as a ballast effect, brings together what is seriously broken. Personality style through the ballast effect is healing of a somebody to become a someone. Healing is evidenced by the *discovery* of style in calling or purpose. Style with calling gives deep meaning for expression as a person of substance. Style of substance is brought into spirituality, by cooking food to bless, wow with photography, repairing things for people with no money; who just need a break, playing music to sooth the soul, using spoken and written words to plant seeds of ideas. Style absolutely is expression that has a lot to do with personality and abilities utilized as gifts. Character presents the exemplar merely by showing up, with the power of presence and authenticity. The Christian shines, is justified, through what they do. Inasmuch, "But wisdom is proved," convincingly Jesus pins it, "to be right by what it does."[265]

Nevertheless, something has to happen, that is, as stated, there is discovery. To discover is to uncover, to detect and catch on. Whatever the ballast effect is for each of us, and the style of making it work,

---

[265] NCV, Luke 7: 35.

might require time and maturation, to find or notice what each person has on the inside waiting to be viewed as redeemed for something worthwhile, expressed in daily life. What the ballast effect does with this discovery of greater potentials as actualities, the person overcomes their possible sense of victimhood. When anyone sees themselves as a victim, they are locked into a destructive past. The past rules the victim when the plow[266] moves forward and they gaze backward. This victimhood cannot not be entirely prevented however. Each of us is a victim, to an extent, taken advantage of from a disturbing opposing otherness. Victims are subjected to events beyond their control, or another person who has nefarious and destructive designs. However, with a shift of perspective, by not seeing ourselves as a victim from deep within the soul, but rather victimized, creates a separation. That is the ballast effect preventing the person from falling apart; gives power to even the odds to stand out and stand tall.

11

Style and Growth. The word "style" is derived from the Latin *stilus* as an instrument for writing, hence our word "stylus" mostly for electronic devices. The stylus enables style, uniquely implemented as a personal expression in writing. The claim, moreover, is for style in Christian spirituality as cited by Paul an apostle. Paul lays it out that we have some contribution to our spirituality: "keep on working to complete your salvation with fear and trembling [regard, respect, appreciation] because God is working in you *to help you* want to do what pleases him."[267] God certainly gives salvation; however, the consequence of salvation is a process of growth or sanctification. Growing spiritually is sanctification, towards a better person than before, which is soul-making. The Christian lives and learns, their new self as God works to complete the person's better self, as that person learns, deeper

---

[266] Luke 9: 62.
[267] NCV, Philippians 2: 12b, 13. Italics added.

spiritual truths are easier to be lived than expected. The direction of such growth, first drives down, graveward, for deep soiled roots, "to leave your old self"[268] or what the *English Standard Version* has, "to put off the old self." The Christian has the imperative to "leave" or "put off" to get rid of the "old self" which is the old identity to make room for the new identity. The new self needs to stand out, finally, from the leftovers of the old self. The process of the leaving, to put off, is to give in without the need to give up. The result is an improved sense of the self. Such is true cooperation with God. During this process, the Christian discovers their unique style of personality expression and authentic carved character. Therefore, the Pelagian hunters need not become exited, to nail another supposed victim to their imaginary style of the Wittenburg door.

The new self reaches upward from its soil of dirty leftovers of the past. The old becomes reconstituted with newness of self. This means deeper understanding about spiritual things, in juxtaposition with a more profound grasp of the self. The mature Christian (regardless of level of advancement), "grows in the way God wants it to grow,"[269] so that the Christian "can mature in your salvation, because you have examined and seen how good the Lord is."[270] Spiritual growth incorporates the style of the person's personality idiosyncrasies to advance in such a "way God wants it to grow" but within the purview of salvation. It means more advanced in spiritual and intellectual, depth. Such Christians have "examined" to deal with pertinent ideas. The overall result is "to grow up in every way into Christ."[271] The Christian stands out, as a someone that can be outstanding in their unique style, a style that does not work against themselves or others. What is denoted here is the sanctification process, which allows for the expression of freedom since "We have freedom now, because

---

[268] NCV, Ephesians 4: 22. Compare Romans 6: 5-7.
[269] NCV, Colossians 2: 19.
[270] NCV, 1 Peter 2: 2
[271] NCV, Ephesians 4: 15.

Christ made us free"[272] (salvation and sanctification). Freedom also is descriptive of God's nature. If God is not free as indicative of his nature, then God is not God. However, freedom is more than Jesus making us free, it involves sanctification as growing has, "God's wisdom, which has so many forms."[273] There are layers in wisdom from God. Wisdom as layers or forms, designed for spiritual deeper experiences to be "mature" in salvation.

Layers within the growing experience are uniquely Christian as a philosophical affirmation about spiritual contents. The intimation for a spirituality is continual or on and off, not continuous or uninterrupted, growth. Sometimes forward, other times staying put on a plateau experience. Staying still, perhaps more often happens on a spiritual plateau where nothing much happens, but eventually, moving forward in growth. That is a crucial concept to grasp, because here is peace with oneself and with God, without throwing everything away due to disbelief. No second-guessing as to what is going on. The old language for this is conversion, which can have an abrupt beginning, although it is a continual salvation event. Hence, soul-making.

12

Soul-making. Soul work is soul-making. Soul work means to be attentive to the internal reality of the presence of who we are. Deep in our constant familiarity, always there, can be identified who we are, is where the work on the soul changes who we are as a person. That constant familiarity of ourselves is not estranged from ourselves. Soul work does not create out of our nothingness, but works with whatever the soul, the internal reality has to present. Soul-making is the making of the soul more than what it was before. We know this when there is more substance, deeper presence, a sort of alteration

---

[272] NCV, Galatians 5: 1.
[273] NCV, Ephesians 3: 10.

or rearrangement that affects the personality, and by extension, the identity and character, through spiritual awakenings. In Psalm 139, the Psalmist like skipping a flat stone over water, regards to what it means to be made by God, only skims over the subject of soul-making; only because the writer has the integrity to admit he doesn't know any better (verse 6). But that was a different time and with limited understanding, when compared to nowadays.

Soul-making digs deep into the dirt, into the roots of the soul or internal reality. Making of the soul is a dirty job that requires wisdom and patience and perseverance. This work gets messy, soiled in roots, to scrape off the psychic junk. Spiritual work is often abrasive. The old self needs to be sandblasted. Away with the dirt that obscures our unknown potentialities, so the light of insight and God's love can shine through personality, all the way through to our character. Poets and novelists have told us that holes and cracks allow the light in, and where there is much light, there is much shadow (examples, Ernest Hemingway, Leonard Cohen, Johann Goethe, respectively).

Like an archeological excavation site, "soul-making" is a common term philosophy and psychology, to say it politely, has "borrowed" what I suspect from published letters of poet John Keats[274]. Soul-making and the archeological site gives concepts of a philosophical dig that goes deep into the layers of soul's spiritual experiences and the layers that make up our history, character and identity. The layers of the soul and the layers of wisdom go together with the greatest ease, for the discovery of deeper personal meanings.

We may have begun life with a soul, with an internal reality, however underdeveloped, uninformed, lacking definition, and underprivileged, but is buried deep in our constant familiarity. The soul is there. Other nametags used for the soul are, consciousness, self, mind, and ego. Kept to the essential, the nametag as self, internal

---

[274] Keats, in a letter to George and Georgiana Keats. John Keats penned the famous line "vale of soul-making" due to interaction with the world of tears. It is an enduring descriptive phrase.

reality, presence, constant familiarity, possibly spirit, denotes soul. It is not advisable as a dogmatic nametag, favored over another. Either way, the lost soul is out of sight and needs to be revealed for the person's own good. The lost soul diminishes the person. However, when the new spiritual life begins, the new self of our personality brings to the surface of our identity, an improved identity and character. However, initially rough it may be. The Christian learns to stand out from the old self and stand in the new self. Sometimes this process of standing, involves two steps forward with a slip of one step backward, but living with the future in mind, moving forward. Perfectionism is not the Christians concern.

Soul-making deals with the spiritual archeological dig into the layers of the personality that shows off what we're made of. However, not everything about our old self is bad or up to no good. Such as the "reasonable nature"[275] mentioned by Paul Tillich. For instance, to be skeptical is a reasonable nature from early life, is enhanced since the salvation event, and God can utilize that idiosyncratic part of nature to grow spiritually. Another example where God utilizes reasonable aspects of our nature is someone who is good with mathematics; banking or accounting as a career to bless other people's existence has long, long-term material effects. Either they control money or it controls them, regardless of amount. Some *need* more financial guidance, which saves their life. The old self with its reasonable nature, still requires a readjustment, such as soul-making, to function effectively as the new self. This is reconstructionism.

What the soul longs for in soul-making is insight. Insight explores for depth of meaning, which begins with a meaningful relationship with God. Those who experience soul-making describe it as a spiritual awakening. Results are noticed in consciousness as if they were asleep and woke up for the first time. Nonetheless, some Christians carry their spiritual longings too far. Some express a tempting desire for their initial spiritual awakening, to have a re-experience of that loving feeling,

---

[275] *The Courage To Be*, p.13.

because it seems to be more alive and relevant. That is a nostalgic feeling for simplicity and is derived from an unwise longing. That nostalgia, in reality, longs for temptation not to be less complicated. Spiritual maturity has maturity because it is experienced with temptation. Temptation, rather, becomes more complicated as the Christian matures in their salvation. The Christian has forgot they are not as easily fooled as they once were. Therefore, this person is using temptation, not to be tempted to sin, but for a return to simpler times. Complication is evidence for spiritual advancement is an actual experience of maturity, and has wisdom not to long nostalgically for simplicity.

Soul-making deals with not a single one of us arrives here ready-made, as if status with identity and character is neatly placed or understood. The good about the unfinished aspect about ourselves is, God likes to work with messy renovation jobs. God, who is complete, cannot undo himself. Therefore, like the adult in the relationship with the Christian, desires to work on the soul to show off the new self. The spiritual Father and Spirit have desire, longs for the best for their spiritual children. After all, we do not refer to the spiritual change or turning to God as a "conversion" for no good reason. We change a room, for instance, and turn it into something improved, which involves a messy renovation.

13

The Christian is God's construction project. Paul explains, "Do not be shaped by this world; instead be changed within by a new way of thinking. Then you will be able to decide what God wants from you; you will know what is good and pleasing to him [God] and what is perfect."[276] We are free to decide whether our secondary primary shaping influence is from the cultural dimension we deal with on a daily routine. That decision requires consciousness, not floating through life. Floating, their life is aimless without direction. Some

---

[276] NCV, Romans 12: 2, context verses 1-3.

of us are floaters. The primary source, to carry the point, of influence is our own independent thought processes as affected by the Spirit of God, which also requires consciousness for greater effect. The wisdom here is "a new way of thinking" that has a direct connection or intellectual attraction to understand "what is good and pleasing to him [God] and what is perfect." What God considers acceptable, will be to our advantage. This reaches into the hub of soul-making.

Since there is a "new way of thinking" the Christian discovers what Paul says next, the context of faith; this is more than an exercise of the intellect stuffing stuff into the head. The "change within" is from an act of faith, but far from a placebo effect. Faith produces a new thinking and reality is the criterion, not a feel-goodism. In verse three Paul continues, "You must decide what you really are by the amount of faith God has given you." Paul says this because of the previous sentence: "Do not think you are better than you are." The point is, faith, and only here, is it a gift although for the purpose of proper evaluation of ourselves. Faith helps to avoid the temptation to over assess our skills and our inherent self-worth, than we ought to. Faith, only here, is given so we Believers can have a faith in ourselves, to have a balanced view of ourselves.

As a caveat, chapter fourteen of Romans deals a bit, with what is arrogance or simplicity between two kinds of Christians. The one Believer is more mature than the other Believer is, as estimated upon each other's level of faith. However, that chapter does indicate some are easily offended over trifling concerns overall. Only the weak in faith merit extra care and attention not to offend. No claim for caution is advised to the strong in faith. Then, in the last verse in the last sentence, Paul specifies, "Anything that is done without believing it is right is a sin." A quick reading, that appears highly subjective, if taken by itself. He is saying be sure what is right or wrong, based upon some investigative discoveries on how to please God. Likewise, someone is not convinced that something is a sin; equally, it is not therefore a sin, since it cannot be understood otherwise. In reality, however, that something may not be a sin to God.

A few comments by Marvin Vincent could help our understanding about the Romans 12: 2 and 3 reference. Vincent explains from the start, "it is not easy to define accurately" since "the line between conceit and sober thinking is not the same for all" because of the variance of faith, each person has. He goes on, "Hence the precise definition of *faith* will be affected by its relation to the differing gifts in ver.6 . . . not be strictly limited to the conception of justifying faith in Christ, though that conception includes and is really the basis of every wider conception. It is faith as the condition of the powers and the offices of believers, faith regarded as spiritual insight, which, according to its degree, qualifies a man to be a prophet, a teacher, a minister, etc., faith in its relation to character, as the only principle which develops a man's tendencies, whether they lead him to mediation and research, or to practical activity." Insofar, "With faith the believer receives a power of discernment as to the actual limitations of his [and her] gifts."[277] What makes sense is that faith is distributed or "given" "assigned" for the *English Standard Version*, but indirectly from God as a secondary result of "a special gift" to acquire a proper and correct view of one's own self.

Furthermore, verse two in this Romans account, with attention for a change in thinking, it is so new, the word for "renewal your mind" (ESV) means to *renovate* or *renovation*. Renewing takes time because it involves soul-making; dig down and tear apart useless soul junk. Psychotherapy may help; it usually takes longer. God doing the soul work often is faster, because God is not concerned about *why* we are a particular way, rather, *how* to get us where we become as God intended. Their spirituality encourages Christians to be rightwise, which means to be a someone with a future. This kind of soul-making has a "new way of thinking," as Paul tells us we can "decide" for ourselves what works for us and not against us or other people. However, we have to be aware, for unexpected discoveries about ourselves; you know, those renovation jobs have their own

---

[277] *Word Studies in the New Testament*, vol.3, p. 154, 155.

unexpected problems. That is when we stand back to deliberate, decide to have see-through vision about the right thing. One thing is certain, renovation as soul-making seems to never end, is a lifetime process. I am led to believe the finished product will be worth it.

After all is said – the study, reading, sorting philosophical ideas from theological ideas – the rubber hits the road and life goes on. How do we take stuff stuffed into the head to make it real, practical, beyond theory? How does one know that the knowledge, understanding, and wisdom acquired for spirituality is not contrived, forced as a by-product with neatly packaged creative ideas? Spirituality is more than just ideas. There has to be faith that growing spiritually changes how we think and why we live through ideas thought. The faith part is to trust God is working in the background. It's not complicated. However, we can make it as complicated as our personality complexes make it. The difference is we give in to God without the need to give up. That is a paradigm shift.

Random Thoughts

1

Paul tells us that the Believer has the power to "destroy the work of God."[278] That is a bit dubious. There has to be a clause, condition, to such an audacious claim. If the deduction follows through, what God accomplishes, a mere person can bring to ruin. On further analysis, what is destroyed is what God has done for the "weak in faith."[279] The weak in faith appears, "if a person believes something is wrong, that thing is wrong for him."[280] That may be an arbitrary and subjective position to take, for it could have consequence for self-inflicted wounds to the soul if they are not "sure in their own minds."[281] Therefore, the weaker Believer has the obligation to inform those around them what they are dealing with, for instance addictions of some sort, as the weaker Believer. The point Paul is making, the mature are not offended, and the offended or weaker, should not force others to exempt themselves from eating or drinking certain stables of nourishment.

---

278 NCV, Romans 14: 20.
279 Ibid, v.1.
280 Ibid, v.14.
281 Ibid, v.5.

2

Jesus is known as The Shepherd, Helper, Savior, and often as a Friend. Jesus is also called the "Lamb of God."[282] To the contemporary ear referring to Jesus as a Lamb, eventually to be killed, then rise from the dead, seems a bit odd, especially when sung in worship songs.

3

Wisdom is disinterested interest. Wisdom is an aloofness and an intuition, by which, a lucid and sane distance from that which is, has an authoritative discernment. Wisdom and discernment do not function effectively unless there is curiosity. (Peace is satisfaction.)

4

Intellectual suicide is recommitted when reason's power is not acknowledged. Evidence for this intellectual suicide is an inability to understand, to connect different ideas that lead to reasonable conclusions. Truth cannot therefore be recognized and knowledge is misused. (Truth and reality do not contradict.)

5

To sense my presence is to feel my soul. Therefore, I have a constant familiarity, not estrangement, but have an actualized self-consciousness. (Materiality and immateriality are integrated.)

---

[282] NCV, John 1: 29. Context, verses 29-36. Compare Isaiah 53; Jeremiah 11: 19, as a short list.

6

Everything real and genuine requires intellectual effort and spiritual effort. Therefore, Christian spirituality puts me on the correct path so that my longings are finally on the right journey, the direction where I am at home with myself, because I am authentic as God intended initiated by Jesus. This is a spirituality experienced philosophically. (Christian spirituality provides confidence.)

7

I have been driving tractor and trailer, big trucks, for 36 years. I am now retired. Most of driving, as a career, has been worthwhile. Work, however, irrespective of what career, needs imputation with a deeper meaning. The greater importance put into the job, as in driving I did, delivering products that made other people's lives better. In reality, I delivered other people's property. Whether that property was steel, wood, soup, to cardboard or adult beverages – whatever it was – the product belonged to someone else, and they were expecting the product to arrive by a specific date or time. These goods in turn cause the improvement in lifestyle, even, in some instances for better health. I further discovered lots of time for reading while loading or unloading trailers, and listening to audiobooks while driving. Style of life becomes improved and blessed. I jested to friends that God saved me a second time from becoming a boring pedantic. It is true what maxims have wisely imparted about doing what you love and it will not feel like work, including, attitude gives a higher altitude to fly better through life.

Therefore, as a driver, I imputed a style into the reason for doing the job. Such an attitude elevates "doing the job" as just a job, as though doing work with a greater purpose and calling. That sense of calling may come naturally, for instance, a medical doctor or a spiritual helper; for the average "worker" takes a concerted shift in perspective. No matter what we do for a living, if we're doing it just for the money, the job will become tedious. Work becomes harder when it is done only for money.

Particularly as Christians, we should not literally see ourselves *just as a*, truck driver, just as a plumber, just as a doctor, just as a crane operator, or just as a teacher or just as a dentist – you get the point. The *just as* mindset diminishes the job, as well, the personal significance of doing the job, and who we are as a person becomes inconsequential. Always a person first, we are more than a label or nametag attached to our shirt, which is attached to our sense of being and what we do for a living. What that instructs us, what we do for a living, moreover, should not define us as a person. If we see ourselves as just a _____, then the job, profession, or career is *just* putting in time and only doing it for the money. I cannot imagine a more degrading and disappointing drag on a condition of being throughout life, let alone a day, than just putting in time on a job. What helps to accomplish a better attitude is from the Bible: "Work *as if* you were serving the Lord, not as if you were serving only men and women."[283] If the Christian has this approach that, there is more to the job than the money or status, personality will not become diminished and our abilities will not sink to be unnoticed. No deeper calling or purpose imputed into what we do for a job, for something greater than we do, we may very much enjoy doing it. Doing work just for enjoyment, also, seems short sighted. All there is then is a nametag, literally and metaphorically. Then, we have been labeled. Yes, money is important, for it brings quality and opportunity, to the meaning of life. However, doing "the job" just for the money[284] alone seems to sell the soul short.

Since, therefore, we are more than a human, just doing something, we can give work a greater meaning with a simple shift of attitude, by giving it a sense of calling and drive, making a difference with a difference. It prevents us from critical analysis that causes the

---

[283] Ephesians 6: 7. Italics added.

[284] Proverbs 30: 8, 9, warns about being poor and having too much. Ecclesiastes 10: 19, what can be accomplished with money. 1 Timothy 6: 10, "love of money" is the cause of "evil."

negative attitude to see ourselves as just another cog in the wheel, even if you are an entrepreneur, or a self-made business individualist. If we want to know from a spiritual point of view, why we are doing what we do, then be curious as to what we leave behind each day when we leave the work behind. Question: As a person, will they be missed? When someone leaves a business as an employer or as either an employee, at the end of the day, change careers, or retire, will that person be missed? The answer will reveal deeper soul-making, or the lack thereof.

8

Intellectual Bigotry. Since the 1960s and early 1970s, I have presented the idea of *intellectual bigotry*. Intellectual bigotry is the use of the intellect to be unintelligent, often with consequence for narrow mindedness. Furthermore, since the 1960s and 1970s, Western culture has entered a Second Dark Age, which intellectual bigotry has given us, as evidence, the thinking commonly known as "political correctness." Bigotry is intellectual regardless of beliefs, which demonstrates how deceptive it can be to frustrate freedom and reason's power.

The intellectual bigot is how they use intellect, a willful use of the thought processes, not only to be narrow minded, but a learned ignorance. It is a willful intention to misuse the intellect to regress learning. Intellectual bigots are often physically and ideologically, pushy; often protesting and megaphone loud with hateful violence about perceived social abuses. A feature commonly noticed by intellectual bigots is their persistent character assassinations of people that express, not just an opposing view, but views that are different from theirs. Often, they have an anti-Israel mindset. I have yet to comprehend why that is, where the dots are connected. From the perspective for character assassinations and to repress opposing views, intellectual bigotry is old anti-intellectualism dressed up wearing masks like terrorist while protesting and coercing free thought by political correct thinking. Intellectual bigotry is new terrorism. It terrors others into silence.

Read publications by old C. S. Lewis, P. J. O'Rourke, Neil Postman, Thomas Sowell, Shelby Steele; especially Camille Paglia, particularly her, *Sex, Art, And American Culture*, and more recent by Sharyl Attkisson, *The Smear* (2017) for a short list of names, but particularly Allan Bloom. Any search on the internet can provide recent authors. Investigate Bloom's *The Closing of the American Mind*. His book was one of the earliest to deal with the subject of a looming new narrow mindedness. Allan Bloom gave his sharp intuitive insight based upon his personal participation from the inside of academe, with its so-called knowers. Bloom, nor the other authors listed, use the term "Second Dark Age" however. The Second Dark Age demonstrates itself more from the mind of those who presume they are the enlightened; in a 100 years or less, people will laugh at their intellectual bigotry as myopic narrow-minded thinking. Whereas, the person who has become a true authentic knower should have an innocent blush for their pervious incorrect buffoonish ideas and their way of unthinking, the lack of analytical thinking.

Allan Bloom explains, "It is open to all kinds of men, all kinds of life-styles, all ideologies. There is no enemy other than the man who is not open to everything."[285] Openness like that is actually closed, for it accepts everything to avoid perceived intellectual limitations. That would be too much to accept! Bloom again, "Openness used to be the virtue that permitted us to seek the good by using reason. It now means accepting everything and denying reason's power."[286] To be open just for the sake to be open without any considerations of the implications, intimates that reason has not been employed. Bloom carries on, "True openness is the accompaniment of the desire to know, hence the awareness of ignorance. To deny the possibility of knowing

---

[285] *The Closing of the American Mind*, p.27.
[286] Ibid, p.38.

good and bad is to suppress true openness."[287] "Thus there are two kinds of openness, the openness of indifference . . . and the openness that invites us to the quest of knowledge and certitude, for which history and various cultures provide a brilliant array of examples for examination."[288] The idea for this second kind of openness means, as he says in the next sentence, "makes interesting every serious student" for which the first is a dismal flirt with knowledge, is how I'd put it. The student in the first openness, "stunts that desire" to "know what is good."[289] To be open with the desire to know because there is the understanding of ignorance, of not knowing, is to be serious. To be serious means to have a dry sense of humor, to be grave-like in weightiness or urgent to dig for the truth. The authentic knower has a dry seriousness, although balanced, just enough, with humor; not everyone gets it however.

Bloom goes on to explain that part of the process of knowing is to doubt and many people are reluctant to doubt. No doubt, that would open their intellectual bigotry and their presumptions to scrutiny. Perhaps, their nothingness and to experience a flat soul may be revealed? However, the real kicker is his next line that has drawn from a deep well of learning: "Prejudices, strong prejudices, are visions about the way things are. They are divinations of the order of the whole of things, and hence the road to a knowledge of that whole is by way of erroneous opinions about it. Error is indeed our enemy, but it alone points to the truth and therefore deserves our respectful treatment. The mind that has no prejudices at the outset is empty. It can only have been constituted by a method that is unaware of how difficult it is to recognize that a prejudice is a prejudice."[290] This is serious stuff, to be prejudiced enough to be gravely serious about the need to be open to truth. Truth is what cannot be otherwise. Yes indeed, 'error is the enemy" but as Bloom says further on, "It is not

---

feeling or commitments that will render a man free, but thoughts, reasoned thought."[291] Boom wants to talk about "reason's power" because it reaches as far as it can go, right into the soul. Meanwhile Bloom pushes the ide further, "Knowledge is the goal; competence and reason are required of those who pursue it. . . .Thus the advantage of the knowers, who want to pursue knowledge, and that of those who do not know, those who want to pursue their well-being, are served simultaneously, establishing a harmony between them. Thus the age-old gulf separating the wise from those who hold power is bridged, and *the* problem of the wise in civil society is solved."[292] Because of anti-intellectualism of the intellectual bigot, skepticism is doubtful that solutions in society are easily solved, as Bloom may suggest. There is too much ignorant violence nowadays. These ideas Bloom put out, I think, is about intellectual bigotry and evidence for the Second Dark Age.

At one level, intellectual bigotry fears or does not care, for the volition to experience the questioning experience. They are not open to be open to learn. The avoidance of layers of the questioning experience for the intellectual bigot intimates. Therefore, they function at an animal level, grubbily reaching for what instinct dictates. Reason and wisdom teaches the human can rise above their animal dictated instincts. The flipside of this second level of bigotry is groupthink, political correct thinking, the collective is more important than the individual. Unless someone has an anathema for groupthink, such people as individuals thinks reasonably for themselves. The result of this second level, a sort of sublevel, is that freedom to think has shifted from the leftist perspective to the rightist perspective. (I speak as a former leftist.) Left has become right and right has become left. Classic liberal thinking has held the avant-garde for new ideas. Whereas now that openness is welcomed with open-minded thinking from the right or conservative perspective. However, the classic liberal will be open

---

[291] Ibid, p,249.
[292] Ibid, pp.261-2.

to where truth leads. It causes curiosity, whether the conservative mind was rather always more open due to its effect to conserve. It is impossible to conserve by being closed. Sustained conservative thinking needs new ideas or it withers away; which it has not. The intellectually free, open, do not resort to intellectual thuggery as the intellectual bigot. Intellectual thuggery prevents debate because the intellectual as a bigot presume they are the supposed enlightened, after all, over the other shmucks with ideas.

Intellectual bigotry weighs in on the process of spirituality and rationalism; frequently are closely associated. Rationalism is the handmaiden to authentic Christian spirituality but not to be identified as spiritual. The association between these two drives, can become destructive. The destruction between spirituality and rationality happens, as we say, a kind of "occupational hazard" occurs between Christian spirituality and the rational. The intellectual bigotry nowadays that works like hand in glove with political correctness is an occupational hazard to all those who desire true openness for debate on Christian spirituality. Christian spirituality is antithetical to intellectual bigotry. To finish with what may sum things up, "Knowledge is not in itself power," confidently Bloom reminds us, "and though it is not in itself vulnerable to power, those who seek it and possess it most certainly are."[293] The adage: where bigots are, so is corruption and the hazard of destruction.

9

Perhaps most Christians have, or ought to have, some working theory or ideas about evil, violence, and the demonic; because these forces are destructive and dangerous and represent, at the very least, an opposing otherness. Whoever has no interest about evil, as violence or the demonic, they are easily fooled and will experience a frustrated existence. Such an individual presumes interaction with evil is normal,

---

[293] Ibid, p.284.

as a constant consistency without a break. That thinking is like not wanting to know what the enemy is doing; a form of ignorance is bliss. Evil and violence, certainly, can be done by anyone, regardless of mature spirituality or its absence. The spiritually mature, more than likely, are unaffected by the demonic, as far as they can realize. They are not ignorant about evil, nor are they obsessed with it.

Paul instructs the Christians, "Repay no one evil for evil, but give thought to do what is honorable in the sight all. If possible, so far as it depends on you, live peaceably with all."[294] As much as possible, attempts for peace, after an evil event and encounter with an evil person, should be possible. Peace causes retaliation to lose its appeal. However, Christians are instructed not to do what is evil. However, with Peter's usual amendment in spiritual matters says, "Beloved, I urge you, as sojourners and exiles to abstain from passions of the flesh, which wage war against you soul."[295] Whatever is assured to work against our better interests, ought to be avoided, as a natural recourse for being a "sojourner and stranger" while living a normal existential life. From Peter's wisdom, the ideas is while living in this world, the mindset may tend towards the temporal and the material pleasures as all there is as passerby Believers. Rather, since they are not only passerby Believers that have big picture optics of reality, they are nevertheless told to "keep your conduct" to such an extent as "honorable" even when accused "as evildoers" since the accusation holds no credibility.

Often when Believers think of violence, the thinking may focus on end time apocalyptic narrative. All the same, attention also needs to listen to what Paul has told Pastor Timothy.[296] Paul provides a litany of mayhem and chaos, the good the bad and the ugly, topping it off with a five word short sentence. We can hear Paul shout, "Stay

---

[294] ESV, Romans 12: 17, 18. NCV, tones it down, "not pay him back by doing wrong" and to do, "your best to live in peace."
[295] ESV, 1 Peter 2: 11. NCV, since they are "foreigners and strangers in this world" they are "to avoid the evil" that is "against your soul."
[296] 2 Timothy 3: 1-9.

away from those people."[297] Some people have that hell-bent violent look in the eye. People like that are not worth having in our lives. I doubt this biblical citation has anything to do with watching a "good" movie with lots of fighting, shooting and making noise, with the added feature of the protagonist wearing their righteous indignation oozing from their character, putting an end to evil. Nothing can go wrong! Good guys, in the movies, always seem to have an over-stock of acquaintance fighting destructive powers, with a dose of righteous indignation that demands putting the boot on the neck of evil.

With respect to the demonic as a subset unto itself, its function is to distort and to destroy. Evil or the demonic (they are so closely knit) seek destruction. While the spiritually minded are attempting to live a better, improved life that builds up, the demonic seeks to tear down, rip apart anything worthwhile or righteous. Paul Tillich pins it: "The image of perfection is the man who, on the battlefield between the divine and the demonic, prevails against the demonic, though fragmentarily and in anticipation."[298] Frequently we win against the demonic, yet, we realize just around the corner, is another battle we will have to confront, another opposing otherness. When it comes to the demonic, Tillich insists, there is always the "divine-antidivine beings" for which, "They are not simply negations of the divine but participate in a distorted way in power and holiness of the divine." The holy becomes unholy and "tragedy does not *aspire* to divine greatness."[299] He goes on, "Whenever *this* is done, the demonic appears. A main characteristic of the tragic is the state of being bind; a main characteristic of the demonic is a state of being split."[300] For Tillich a main point to grasp is the demonic seeks "distortion." "Distorted spirit is still spirit; distorted holiness is still holiness."[301] Distortion is a form of destruction. Destruction leaves no

---

[297] Ibid, v.5.

[298] *Systematic Theology*, vol.3, p.241.

[299] Ibid, vol.3. p.102.

[300] Ibid, vol.3, p.103.

[301] Ibid, vol.3, p.375.

false impression what is distorted. To distort is to twist out of place. To destroy is to lay something to waste. Twisted and wasted are the markings of the demonic.

The demonic shows its weakness by what it hates. What it hates, it seeks to distort with pseudo-spirituality by imitation, namely, to distort authentic spirituality and spiritual growth. What Tillich has to advise, "Growth in Spiritual freedom is first of all growth in freedom from the law. This follows immediately from the interpretation of the law as man's essential being confronting him in a state of estrangement. The more one is reunited with his true being under the impact of the Spirit, the more one is free from the commandments of the law."[302] The demonic, therefore, by pseudo-spirituality does the unholy act to cut off freedom from the center of the personality, as a free expression of the personality. Another way to say this, when there is no freedom then rules rule, which brings repression of the personality. The more freedom is experienced from burdensome unnecessary rules, the greater realization is evident about the power of freedom. The power of freedom is friendly. The destructive power from the demonic is not friendly; however, it is not far removed.

After all, it is more than mere fortuitous creative writing on Paul's part, when he instructed Believers with the tone of wise caution. He says, "until we all attain to the unity of the faith and of the knowledge of the Son of God, to mature manhood [personhood], to the measure of the stature of the fullness of Christ."[303] Until then, some childish styles of thinking will persist like uncontrolled waves preventing maturity.

---

[302] Ibid, vol. 3, p.232.
[303] ESV, Ephesians 4: 13, context, verses 11-16.

10

Mistakes are not *necessarily* sins. That seems obvious. Is every sin a mistake? Perhaps normal pleasures are gained because of a sin. However, though fortunate results due to a sinful act, acts full of sin, does not give the license to cause *every* sin to be justified. Sinful acts overflow with self-centeredness. Therefore, sin so God's grace proliferates? In addition, to repeat the sin? Such a person does not understand the power of God or the power of sin: both will destroy the soul when no turning away from the desire to sin constantly repeated, again with the same sin. Jesus tells us, "Don't be afraid of people, who can kill the body but cannot kill the soul. The only one you should fear is the one who can destroy the soul and the body in hell."[304] God will turn loose people to their own self-destruction, where the consequences of sin finish off the job. God does not directly destroy in hell; people send themselves by their sins, and God certainly is able to destroy evil. Jesus is saying that fear God over and above hell. Think hell is tuff? Hell *is* the capability to lose all sight of eternity. Hell will destroy or perish completely any opportunity for eternal life, since it means to lose eternal life. To destroy is to lose since hell is the opposite of true life.[305] Therefore, in the long run, every sin is a mistake, however fortunate the immediate gains imagined.

---

[304] NCV, Matthew 10: 28.
[305] Compare Matthew 10: 39, "hold on to their lives will give up true life;" – John 12: 25 has the additional feature, "true life forever."

AFTEREFFECT

PRIMARY 1

1

To borrow a line from Alan Jones and to sum up, "God's great gift to me is to enjoy me so much that I can be at home with myself."[306] To be at home with our true self that is our new self from the fragmented ruins of the old self, because of salvation, is identical to the mature independence gained, earned, between an adult parent and their child. The first gift may be salvation, but an aspect of it is a second order gift is sanctification, which has, as its own way of giving, is to be at home with whom God has intended for us to be. It would be great to leave this at that. However, to have a relationship with God is the other aspect of relationship Christians contend with: besides God's love and peace, is discipline and correction, what is either directly or indirectly from God. To be at home with God means living under God's house rules and that means some corrections.

2

There is no complaint about God proving his love, in fact, it is welcomed. However, when discipline and correction is involved, then some people become discouraged or feel estranged from God.

---

[306] *Passion For Pilgrimage*, p.163.

Understanding the relationship with God, indeed, outcome some discipline and correction, not just love; which should be expected. A crucial aspect of growing spiritually involves discipline and correction, not only love and being at one with God kind of feeling. James Hillman, on a slightly different subject but makes sense here, "Until the culture recognizes the legitimacy of growing down, each person in culture struggles blindly to make sense of the darkenings and despairings that the soul requires to deepen life."[307] It is from those dark times with existential despair that many sense God is disciplining and dishing out corrections. That may be true, or it is the run of things. Things happen. On the other side, many Christians understand that "darkenings and despairings" are not entered "blindly" because it is accepted that the soul requires insight, wisdom, becoming authentic, to be renewed[308] in the mind. This means to experience a "growing down" in order to grow up. A huge aspect of growing up is to attain an independent mindset. Does God discipline and correct so that we would grow up and become more independent? Does spiritual maturity have the mark for an independent-dependent relationship? If we refuse to grow up spiritually with some intellectual astuteness, what are the consequences, what does that look like?

3

The letter for the "Hebrews" in the New Testament is mostly comprised to suggest one group of immature Christians. The original recipients of the letter were somewhat slow on the intellectual draw. They were more mature at one time but became lazy and could not bother to "know the difference between good and evil."[309] That is a bad place to be. To understand the 'difference" between "good and evil" is the minimum elementary spiritual depth. What is going on

---

[307] *The Soul's Code*, p.43.
[308] Romans 12: 2, ESV, "be transformed by the renewing of your mind."
[309] NCV, Hebrews 5: 14.

with these Christians is there are two kinds of Christians dealt out two kinds of discipline, from God. The more advanced, mature, are disciplined more from a nudge by encouragement if they catch on fast enough. The less advanced, immature, will be disciplined by going through sufferings with the intent they will catch on, if they do at all. Moreover, it is highly improbable that every Christian referred to in the Hebrew letter, were only the less advanced or only from the more advanced, group of Christians; there must have been a mixture. Let us work through this assertion.

From chapter five some Christians, the *more advanced, mature,* became "slow to understand"[310] since they were "not ready for solid food"[311] even though they "should be teachers"[312] but were not up for the task. As it confirms in verse 14, nonetheless, these Christians were "mature enough" or not "unskilled,"[313] therefore, not entirely incapable on the use of "discernment" as a "practice to distinguish good from evil."[314] This is more descriptive of a more spiritually advanced, mature Christian, although they became "slow to understand." This group of Christians were disciplined and corrected with the nudge of encouragement, shamed into becoming what they were capable of performing. As the writer goes on to encourage them with a verbal nudge: "So let us go on to grown-up teaching."[315] That nudge of encouragement, to get their process of maturation out from a state of stagnation, stalled in neutral and mediocrity, is told to advanced, mature Christians.

The other Christians are *less advanced, immature,* and received a greater discipline and correction. This group is reminded they had forerunners in the faith, therefore, they had examples on "remove from our lives anything that would get in the way and the sin that so easily

---

[310] Ibid, v.11, ESV, "it is hard to explain, since you are dull."
[311] Ibid, v.12, ESV, "You need milk, not solid food."
[312] Ibid, v.12, ESV, "you ought to be teachers."
[313] ESV, v.13.
[314] ESV v.14.
[315] NCV, Hebrews 6: 1, context 1-3.

holds us back."[316] These Christians held on to useless psychological weight, and could not let go, especially of clingy things that causes actual sins. They held on to their needy way of living. It is as though disciplined and corrected, but keep on allowing such reasons for the discipline and correction to "get in the way" of progress. However, these Christians are encouraged to "hold on through your sufferings" those reoccurring troubles, since they consider that "God is treating you as children"[317] and that "children are disciplined"[318] in a specific manner, "so we will have life."[319] If there is no discipline and correct for such Christians, they acquire a bratty attitude and God becomes the Candy Man with all the sweetheart deals. In a way, such Christians are diminished or "illegitimate."[320] However, when such Christians "have learned from it" they will "have peace."[321] The intellectual takeout is the less advanced, immature, have a difficult time to obtain peace. Peace is contingent to catch on to their situation. If they do not catch on, sins easily get in the way to prevent maturity. Otherwise, life becomes a repetitive treadmill.

The mature Christian rather should have the discernment that God is working in the background to orchestrate some events, but for which, others involved have no evil intent and often are completely unaware. We must discern whether discipline and correction is from God, or, the misuse of correction from a destructive disciplinarian more concerned that rules rule, or it is a troublesome force from a snarky bully. Discipline and correction as a counterbalance from God never seeks to destroy or harm.

---

[316] Ibid, 12: 1, context 1-11, ESV, "lay aside every weight and sin which clings so closely."
[317] Ibid, 12: 7.
[318] Ibid, v.8.
[319] Ibid, v.9.
[320] ESV, v.8.
[321] NCV, v.11.

4

In spite of former divines that have gone before us — we read their books, have their examples — the new spiritual life in Christianity, lived through the new self, is a sojourn not traveled alone, although it is experienced individually and personally. God with the Christian, between them, deal with their own stuff, on what is going on between each of them. That is none of our business. As Peter was a bit whinny concerning John's affairs, Jesus turns to Peter and says, "If it is my will that he remain until I come, what is that to you?"[322] Occasionally, we may notice a fellow Believer dealing with personal growing pains, however it requires an astute discernment whether to leave them to their searching or get involved. Not always easy to step back and get out of the way so God can accomplish what we often cannot.

5

Paraword philosophical diagnostic questions: What does the new self look like as we mature spiritually? After we are a brand new self, does newness ever become old, usual and regular? Are we pushed forward or pulled forward in our spiritual way of being? Peter has a fascinating lead to those questions. Questions are connected to what answers our longings. He pins it down, "As new born babies want milk, you should want the pure and simple teaching. By it you can mature in your salvation, because you have already examined and seen how good the Lord is."[323] The ESV for this verse is more precise with a sarcastic bite, as a snap from a whip: "Like newborn infants, long for the pure spiritual milk, that you may grow up into salvation — if indeed you have tasted that the Lord is good." The Believer is obligated to investigate, to be a detective into what it

---

[322] ESV, John 21: 22, NCV, "that is not your business."
[323] NCV, 1 Peter 2: 2, 3.

means to be saved in their salvation experience, and be mature about it. To be mature about, suggests openness to what is discovered and own it and work with it for greater maturity. Therefore salvation has more to offer than the initial experience of being saved. The salvation event is experienced by growing up into a mature salvation experience, which is, a new reputation as a new identity understood as the new self that replaced the fragmented old self. The subject here ultimately is sanctification. Sanctification is the process of soul-making or growing spiritually, to become an authentic person. This means to yield to that process, which means to give in without the need to give up, because the results are through spiritual effect from the Spirit of God. It is far from a simple process. Because, it is interested in mature development from where the Christian is at, with their potentialities, to where they will become in actualities, as a person. Sanctification, by definition, gives personal style of presence to each Christian as evidenced in personality and in character development, because that is where the growth process comes from. As Peter tells us specifically, such a maturation is about learning from sound, thorough, reliable, and good or right "teaching" which the mature "already examined" so they get it that there is more to salvation than is first initially experienced. Otherwise, what is the point of salvation, just to give eternal life?

6

In a nutshell, sanctification is the process of growing spiritually which has a direct affect for improvements upon the Christian's personality and character. It is a process of learning biblical truths with their attached philosophical curiosity, which in turn helps to grow spiritually and intellectually. The process that involves sanctification has a pull and a push feature to the growth it seeks to accomplish as a new condition of being. Because now the pull is from the Spirit and the push is from the new self. The new self has a restored relationship with the Spirit of God[324] and the Spirit of Jesus,[325] which is the Holy Spirit.[326] Often there is the mixture, to go on, of a pull towards personal future development, or, there is a push from a present condition of maturity that has the inclination to lean towards further future development. Sometimes the future is pulling, then, other times there is a sense of pushing. The pull/push experience is the work of the Spirit. The Spirit's results, for the new self, are connected to the Christian's personal style. Consequences show unique spiritual interests for that person. The point is, the Christian has the mindset that sanctification as a process of growing spiritually and intellectually, is the evidence that God through his Holy Spirit is in a new relationship with the Christian.

7

To sanctify is to give that something an alteration, to consecrate and make it hallowed, holy. The unholy becomes holy. In the process of sanctification of spiritual maturity and intellectual astuteness, the hallowed ground from which such growth springs[327] or flows as Jesus assured, is from the soul or internal reality of the personality. Growing and maturing encourages personal style and presence developed within personality. This is the results from the salvation event, to alter, improve, or advance, the salvation event towards a greater mature experience. To grow spiritually becomes a holy event because the growth is holy; the purpose is for a holy cause.

The purpose of salvation is to restore the estranged relationship between humans and God, which is to know God – for those who take advantage of the salvation – in an intimate personal relation with eternal practical result. The result is for the Believer to become holy. Salvation is often described as regeneration, justification, however,

---

[324] Romans 8: 9
[325] Philippians 1: 19.
[326] 1 Corinthians 6: 11.
[327] John 4: 13.

sanctification has its own category. Except that, regeneration and justification are specific aspect of salvation. Sanctification is the specificity of salvation that identifies itself as the process of growing spiritually, which includes the development of intellectual astuteness, all for the purpose of holiness. The reason that extra clarification of the intellectual quality, there is no other demarcation to determine to one's self, that spiritual maturation is an objective estimation. Feelings are not objective thoughts. Spiritual maturation, therefore, cannot not be assessed by subjective feelings. Assessment is evidenced from holy living, connected to the new way of thinking from the new self; everything for spiritual growth has its antecedent back to God.

Sanctification is understood from Scriptural ideas. However, Paul mentions that the Believer has died in a spiritual meaning, to their old self through Jesus as the Christ and therefore, "We know that our old life died with Christ on the cross so that our sinful selves would have no power over us and we would not be slaves to sin. Anyone who has dies is made free from sin's control."[328] "You were made holy, and you were made right with God in the name of the Lord Jesus Christ and in the Spirit of our God."[329] Sanctification shows salvation further as an experience that transcends it as an event. The self-evidence or showing off is for deeper in meaning. This deeper meaning is holiness, more than justified or made right and regenerated or reconnected, to God, but with the feature of holiness. Holiness is not sinless whatsoever, as if never at fault. Holiness is rather a condition of being with the propensity to sin less.

Paul Tillich describes sanctification as a transformation of growing spiritually: "Sanctification, or the process toward Spiritual maturity, conquers loneliness by providing for solitude and communion in interdependence. A decisive symptom of Spiritual maturity is the power to sustain solitude. Sanctification conquers introversion by

---

[328] NCV, Romans 6: 6, 7, context 1- 14. Compare Galatians 2: 20; Ephesians 4: 22-24.

[329] NCV, 1 Corinthians 6: 11.

turning the personal center not outward, in extroversion, but toward the dimension of its depth and its height."[330] Moreover, what that further means there must be "awareness, freedom, and relatedness" which leads to "This implies that sanctification is not possible without a continuous transcendence of oneself in the direction of the ultimate – in other words, without participation in the holy."[331] Tillich uses "participation" where I use "relationship," both refer to regeneration. None of this sanctifying work happens unless there is involvement with the New Being (Tillich), the new approach introduced by Jesus, what I refer as the new condition of being or the new way of being, which is opposed to the old condition of being. That may not be exact to Tillich's meaning of New Being, although it involves much more, "The New Being is new in so far as it is the undistorted manifestation of essential being within and under the conditions of existence."[332] Briefly, sanctification's function is to encourage growth beyond our neediness, "but toward the dimension of its depth and its height."

8

Salvation and spiritual maturation only occurs with some intellectual astuteness. For, there is no other method to ascertain we are growing spiritually. The Christian may have more than enough love and have the patience and wisdom to overlook a fault in others, but that does not specify maturity that has spiritual insight. However, distinctive feature of salvation regardless of intellectual seriousness or spiritual sensitivity as a natural ability, salvation gives a new definition as the

---

[330] *Systematic Theology*, vol.3, p.234.

[331] Ibid, vol.3, p.235.

[332] Ibid, vol.2, p. 119, see p.121, Jesus is "bearer of the New Being;" pp.176-180, where New Being provides "participation" (regeneration), "acceptance" (justification), "transformation" (sanctification). Also, Spiritual Presence, vol.3. p.144, the Spirit is in Jesus "without distortion" though lived within the human condition; p.283, "The Spiritual Presence is the Presence of God under a definite aspect." Aspect is the "human spirit" and "everything" of "the spirit."

new self. To have sense of a brand new self, is the rock bottom line of Christian spirituality – without it, we do not have that spirituality – only a pseudo-Christian spirituality. The new self, as described from the Bible, is to be a new creation.

From one of the most concise popular Bible verse for Christians throughout recent history is, "If anyone belongs to Christ, there is a new creation. The old things have gone; everything is made new!"[333] Not understanding what that verse means, is to be on the outside looking in. The average somebody becomes a someone; because of salvation a someone is a new self. Not only is the person as Christian "made new" but also "everything is made new." There is now a new frame of reference, a new fresh way of looking at things, life is being in a new condition of being as holy; it is as though a new style actually makes sense and is a possibility, not out of reach to be holy. The person is a new creation because they became what they were not before. The unholy become holy. Such a Christian can identify everything about themselves as a new identity.

Is everything made brand new? Since there is a constant familiarity at the baseline of personality, the "reasonable nature" (Tillich) must not be transformed, although it is seen with a new perspective. Furthermore, this verse from Paul informs us that, first, because of the effect of being made new, secondary, every aspect of our constant familiarity can be seen from a new objective perspective that the Christian is not estranged or schizophrenic or disordered. At one level of this new perspective makes it possible to notice details. On another level of this new perspective, changes in the person's life are evidenced as real changes, not from an occluded perspective that is disordered. The Christian can notice clearly themselves from a new angle to compare where some aspects have been changed in personality, character, and identity; possibly as God sees them. The new perspective of two levels allows the Christian to view themselves objectively. So, the "everything" has two layers to it. Besides, Paul also

---

[333] NCV, 2 Corinthians 5: 17. ESV, "if anyone is in Christ, he is a new creation."

wrote to Christians they had the obligation 'to put off the old self"
so thereby "be renewed in the spirit of your minds" then they would
know experientially what it was like "to put on the new self, created
after the likeness of God in true righteousness and holiness."[334] This
reminds what Paul said a few paragraphs earlier, "you may be filled
with all the fullness of God."[335] As a brand new self, the Christian is
a restyled creation in the sense of obtaining a new original formation,
since they are starting all over for the first time. To become a new self
also appears to be a once in a lifetime deal, a one-time event; not to
be confused, there is a hint from the Bible that multiple, consecutive,
new creation experiences could occur in sanctification. Meanwhile,
there is always deeper soul work for soul-making!

9

Somewhere I read the old Greeks claimed the musical lyre (harp)
needed to be fine-tuned in order to sound like a lyre was intended to
be heard; in the same way so does the soul. So they argued the needs
of the soul must be finely tuned from time to time. Our soul needs to
be tuned up, timed, adjusted and attuned. The only way to do that is
to work with word power tools and parawords that can feed the soul
with insights into the soul's longings. What we give most attention
to, we become attuned to, attend to, thereby paying attention to
what kind of spiritual food nourishes us in regard to our new style,
causes spiritual strength to be an actuality, beyond theory. Paying
attention feeds the soul with the only kind of food it can digest:
insight. Therefore, philosophically, look for words that encourage,
that give the courage to be, for they will also heal and produce from
their cornucopia a bounty for authentic soul-making. Spiritually,

---

[334] ESV, Ephesians 4: 22-24, context 17-24. NCV, "made to be like God." See v.13, "fullness of Christ."
[335] Ibid, 3: 19.

therefore, it is the process of sanctification, growing, which means to give in, to God, without the need to give up.

10

I have not attempted to write an academic work. "Know your limitations," people like to remind us, even when it comes from the movie character Dirty Harry. However, neither what is presented is mere mental gymnastics designed for a good intellectual workout. Most intellectual ideas ought to be applied, for daily living, nevertheless, some pragmatism helps for the long haul. Ideas that can hit the road running are practical resolutions. I gathered ideas from Christian spirituality and from my life as a Christian. However, like many ideas about Christian spirituality, they make more sense after the fact – while hitting the road running – living practically, as a spiritual practice. Reading the Bible and biblical concepts, in practice, causes spiritual experiences to be confirmed, as beyond the head. Christian spirituality, for sure, can be caught up in more theory than practice, causing pedantism, is an occupational hazard of spirituality. Yet, theory cannot be discarded – for practical reasons. That is the point: eventually, a theory should work, be applicable for the daily run of life. Christian spirituality, is a reasonable spirituality, that becomes more than stuff stuffed into the head. It reaches down and digs around in the soul, to hit hard for soul-making. The person's life is changed, is under construction, rearranged and renovated. However, the crucial difference is spirituality does not become an occupational hazard. Ultimately, it isn't that complicated. When a fellow Christian appears somewhat out of place, maybe they are at that renovation stage that gives an indication of what is going on, but not too sure how it will look later on. Renovation work requires patience with a truckload of wisdom.

PRIMARY 2

1

I want to tell a story about an old book, and use it as a metaphor for instruction on a spiritually changed life that everyone longs for.

In my library bookcase there is this old, not too ragged, but antique looking book. The exterior cover attached to the spine is a bit loose. Other than that, it is in good condition. It isn't worth much in terms of hard cold cash. Perhaps $20.00 at a used bookstore. It is one of those books that seem difficult to ignore. There's no alluring picture on its cover, as books today. Yet, it has that appearance that can cause the curious mind to wonder if the book is asking, "What are you waiting for? Open me up. See what happens." Just to set it straight, paper books do not speak out loud. Anyway, it has that authoritative commanding appearance with authenticity. Whenever, for sure, we roll our eyes over a book's cover to thumb through it, we truly are listening for the sound of the click from the ratchet set of word power tools, parawords attached – designed to help make life easier and improved. The click of the sound from word power tools is the sound of wisdom. We want to catch a concept of perception, as it offers insights. The sound of word power tools has what it takes to convince and encourage, so that we can be at home with ourselves, especially as an act of maturing in salvation. Through words, the mind's eye sees what the soul hears. Those two are in unison and the knowledge they embody brings us back repeatedly, to the power of the word.

The old book is a collection of pieces of poems. Its title, *Beauties Of Modern British Poetry*, with no date. Nelson's website has it published in 1871, in Edinburgh. The edited segmented poems are from the best parts from the best-liked poems from the best authors of the day. Big sounding names that have the weight of authenticity from the likes as Byron, Bowring, Coleridge, Cowper, Keats, Scott, Wordsworth, with a host of lesser luminaries, at least for me.

The old book's covers are hard, made to last. The exterior of the book's hard surfaces are to protect its softer internal reality, its very soul and constant familiarity. The middle of the book is neatly arranged letters from the alphabet – creation itself into words – stare back with old stored wisdom wedged between each line. The glue and thread from the book's spine has not turned to dust – yet. Because it was designed to last, it has holding power. It has the appearance of completeness and authenticity and power: perfect perfection, full of divine inspiration. You perhaps, have seen similar books for yourself. The cover has raised etchings, curves, grooved decorative lines with parts of the cover's raised surface somewhat rubbed off due to age, mostly, from readers removing it from its resting place between other books. The book has dusty character, carved with style and presence.

The pages of this book are the old style or the academic book style, with wide margins for notes. It even has the aroma of being old with its pages in sepia color. In spite of its title, it has gleaned from that period referred to as the "Modern Age" around 1500 to 1800. The book's contents may have some forgotten poems with long dead poets, yet, some are read today. Talk about lasting power. Cynically speaking, the term "modern" conjures up definition as relative. The preface assures any reader that the authors were picked like fruit from the tree of knowledge, with interest, poems noted for their own style of power and lasting greatness. Style of power and lasting greatness are not always the latest new ideology or material object or electronic device. Likewise, we really do not know what will have lasting greatness until after the expiry date has come and gone. There are hints of greatness, there is a sense, a particular object or idea will outlast its inventor. Style of power lasts since it must have a universal appeal and simultaneously a universal quality; a combo deal tested over time and must be applicable and practical for any generation and any culture or society.

Christian spirituality has lasting style of power. The spirituality offered is timeless, has universal applicability for any culture; it is not locked in its own historical backyard like a junkyard dog. Here we are, thousands of years after its initiation; still breathing life to the meaning of personal lives. It would otherwise become irrelevant and useless, tossed to the dusty backyard of its past. The form of its expression often becomes irrelevant however, when that form overtakes its substance; then rules rule, and its spirituality becomes brittle, its life sucked out by natural existential concerns. It can be a caricature of its greatness and easily blows away with every wind of new ideas. Examples: a worship service must only be a certain way, wear just right cloths, drive the wrong car, hooked on groupthink/political correctness, speak in Christianese, content with the bored again or status quo – if these are more important, then form means more than substance. Substance, on the other side, is what stands firm from the essential characteristic of a person or a concept or a material object. Substance that can hold up, with a strong firm stand is what form needs. Form gives formation – it is not entirely off. Substance does need a particular form therefore. Substance holds and becomes what it is filled, and has style regardless of form. Like presence, substance stands out.

Beauties Of Modern British Poetry has been resting, truthfully, more ignored on my bookshelf for most of the time. It is relaxing, waiting to be picked up. As stated, I found that book in a used bookstore, approximately twenty years ago. I peak into it occasionally, looking for gems of insight to feed the soul. Rarely has it been opened without that old book smell to pass the nose. Recently, however, I opened it to discover something I missed before. Between its pages was a gift from a previous reader. The other reader treated the book with love and care, comprising style with interest. I know this by thumbing over the book's pages to be surprised to find, 20 years later, squeezed firmly are five thin tiny beautiful remnants of clothe cut into bookmarks. These frayed pieces that remind of a soul, were cut to size, just for this book. That's thinking with style. Soul-making by reading truths cuts the excess from the internal reality, the soul.

These five pieces of frayed clothe looked as though they also were around a long time; faded in color. The pervious reader was creative and frugal. Those tiny pieces of clothe were placed between pages where ideas had meant something more than just modern stuff stuffed into the head, meanings reached into the heart or soul. Good ideas are timeless. Those pieces of clothe used as bookmarks are pleasing to the eye, smooth and soft yet strong, even after time has passed. They have a future. I did not toss them away. Likely these pieces of clothe connected other pieces of ideas from other pages.

Did those ideas nourish the soul of that reader? These pieces of bookmarks were pressed firmly between pages, where words as power tools fall out to fill the mind. Feed the soul and newness is created. Those words on those pages said something to someone, where today time has completely forgot. I can only imagine what the reader was longing for. Marking and underling words, as we do, would do harm to the beauty of the book. Therefore, unknown to me, I cannot determine what the reader noticed. What were they paying attention to? What was precious to their soul? Maybe we should underline words in our books, for posterity! They could receive insight into our own soul. After all, a personal library is consciousness made visible.

I found something else in that old book besides bookmarks and wisdom. It was nearly undetectable, for it blended into the words of the paper. Squeezed between the pages, was one tiny tapered pointy green leaf at both ends, except the one end has the remains of the stem, but the other end more to a point. The middle of the leaf is a little broader. The leaf was a quickly used bookmark.

Now, the leaf is off brown from the page's paper. The appearance, recalls back Egyptian papyrus. This leaf has a woodgrain appearance with webbed veins that once carried its nourishment. Its appearance also reminds of a flat fossilized feather. It was dead and brittle. But the leaf looked amazing. It is very susceptible to damage. Beauty indeed is pure wholesome pleasure and often, susceptible to easy damage. Age can be ruined, damned. I did not have the heart to toss it either, as if it had no meaning. Maybe in heaven we will look middle-aged, so that everyone can recognize each other. In heaven, we need to be recognizable, have recognition. Sometimes we *hear our hear-t*.

When we hear our heart, we can hear the hunger pangs of what the soul longs for.

Looking at the leaf, I imagined a distant reader comfortably relaxed under a tree, shaded, from the heat of the midday sun. While reading, they could have been mindlessly fingering this tiny leaf. Perhaps they were summoned hurriedly, quickly finish reading and place the leaf between two pages. They run off only to forget the leaf packed there for remembrance. In a needful style, the leaf looked better with age. The leaf was able to show off its presence through the style of new color, although with its unique markings for character made more visible. Dryness often shows off the lines and markings of a carved character. The leaf, no doubt, has character and presence just as the book. The leaf borrowed from the book. Christian spirituality borrows from context of The Book, but receives the content from its Author. There is a metaphor here: we take the characteristics of the books we read, especially from the Bible. Bible reading has that style to read us *as* we read it. Which makes the Bible more than a manual for life. Do not judge a book by its cover, we are told.

Primary 3

1

The mature Christian understands they do not exactly borrow, as the leaf did, from everything, as if we were predetermined without a freedom. Another reason, we do not even borrow from God. The Christian more exactly receives from God, because God wants to give. God uses our faith to accept the gift of salvation, which does not make it a debt owed to God. To make that claim, is to force an understanding the Scriptures do not claim, what does not exist in print or intimation. Those that claim Jesus paid a debt that the unwashed, therefore owe, turn salvation into another form of works or performance driven transformation; it means to turn grace into a graceless grace. The Bible does not state anywhere that a sinner owes a debt because of sin. God rather accepts our repentance because of our faith as New Believers. There is absolutely no performance driven debt payed for what Jesus accomplished for redemption and sanctification. Otherwise, salvation would not be a gift. True enough, Jesus paid with his life the price of sin. However, that does not create a debt owed; rather the Believer is grateful for the offer of grace. The debt owed posits an erroneous philosophical concept about a theological idea.

The proposition that Jesus paid for our sins is an unfortunate use of words. Rather it means that Jesus gave himself for our sins. Therefore those that say since Jesus paid, has created a philosophical mistake, which craters, hollows out correct theological ideas about salvation. It forces an unnatural interpretation of what the Bible teaches about salvation and what Jesus accomplished. For further information about a debt owed philosophy, as examples, see these two websites, christianhistoryinstitute.org, and, carm.org. The first website has an excellent conversational presentation between these two monks, Anselm (1033-1109) and Boso (1124-1136). It was Anselm who first conjured up this crazy idea about a debt owed, commonly called the "Penal Substitution" theory of atonement. Anselm was not a wingnut, but a formidable thinker for theological and philosophical ideas. It should be noted, early Christians did not dream up the nutty idea that we owe God. Christians in debt to God? It is fallacious reasoning showing Christians as worse off than needs to be. Why do that?

The Christian has faith for their improvements and spiritual maturation, faith to have faith for the process and relationship with the Spirit of God, faith for spiritual growth with its intellectual necessity for astuteness. The Christian does not have to die to show off character and presence, as the leaf in the book had to. Accordingly, the work of the Spirit is for the person as a Christian, becomes alive. What becomes an actuality is the Christian becomes alive, as God full of his life. Except, God allows for our own style of fully being alive. Which relates to our own specific developmental needs. The

Christian has a full sense of life as it relates to their actual personality idiosyncratic traits. To be alive as God is alive, or perfectly full of life, although, is fragmented, split, at times, is due to our existential condition of being. Unlike God who cannot be imperfect, who cannot be but himself at all times full of himself, for us sin gets in the way, or we say something really stupid, out loud, and then our style becomes frayed. Because, fortunately, forgiveness for the Christian is a given, since Jesus already has offered forgiveness – there is power to overcome sin and hopefully do it with style.

We do not need to denigrate those who are chronologically younger. They are not aged however green, unripe, inexperienced – beyond redemption (there's an old phrase) – unable to make insightful judgments about that which matters. Some people may otherwise always be *un*-becoming. When we are clued out, not thinking clearly, it means the thread used to bring together ideas is frayed, not efficient. To be clued in, means to thread together. That which matters is about good universal ideas that have lasting style of power. Lasting style of power has authority for it is characterized by authenticity. When authenticity is absent from an older person, inevitably there is an undeveloped self or soul without authority. An antique book may appear knowledgeable with stored wisdom however, unlike the book, the older green person may appear knowledgeable, wise and well used, even very experienced, but something is missing. The ingredient missing is wisdom, because the soul has not experienced soul-making. They have not paid attention to attend to their soul's longings. Greenness lacks personal authority, nor does it have authenticity, although these point to potentials.

The Christian who can be at home with themselves, without being neurotic or disordered about it, will likewise be at home with God. They will identify with their identity. They will have personal authority to authorize their life with authenticity, and, they are at peace with God and themselves. The longing to be at home with their own sense of self as a new self, as a past spiritual event that has already occurred; is the evidence of a mature salvation and not feeling guilty for not wanting to be guilty anymore. Still, such a Christian still has another longing, a longing belonging to their constant familiarity, as an ordinary reason for the condition of being. There is satisfaction that is more like being contentedly discontented; they will accept more but are satisfied nonetheless. The next longing is to be an explorer, to search for deeper understanding about Christian spirituality. Remember what Jesus said about someone that has insight into spiritual curiosities and soul work? Jesus believed such a person "brings out both new things and old things he has saved"[336] or to put it another way, "brings out of his treasure what is new and what is old" (ESV). With poetic license, to put words into the mouth of Jesus, "Yeah but, do it with style."

From the Old Testament, a line that sparkles bright with insight, shed on the idea Jesus is getting across. Its writer pens, "But the path of the righteous is like the light of dawn, which shines brighter and brighter until full day."[337] The Christian from their depth of insight draws out new ideas because of the old ideas, and what they have to teach springs from the soul of experience and what they have learned. Their knowledge causes their understanding to become brighter each time they explore for new and deeper ideas. The bright idea and the wise person's "path" or the style of living, beyond mere existing, shines with confidence in truth. Such a person has a gradual illumination that digs deeper for understanding that slowly becomes brighter as they grow spiritually. Whereas sudden flashes of insight causes blindness where tangents steer off course.

The wise become brighter to have a positive effect for mature spiritual soul work that even impresses God. The dark opposite from the next verse crackles with judgment, a discerning assessment, "The way of the wicked is like deep darkness; they do not know over what they stumble."[338] The wise and the rightwise will likewise shine

---

[336] NCV, Matthew 13:52b.
[337] ESV, Proverbs 4: 18, context, vs.10-19. Compare John 12: 35, 36.
[338] Ibid, v.19.

brighter, all in good time. Anyhow, that intimates further paths for our sojourn.

2

Another turn on the thinking lathe: To posit that if a person went out in a blaze of glory, flares with the burn of flashes of insight, lead nowhere. The person burns bright with illumination; they burn out before their time. Recall Paul an apostle, when he was on his last missionary tour? It is certain his life ended and God's work through him in Roman, where he died a death we are not sure of. Paul probably died at the expense of a blood sport. It is concluded he died some sort of martyr's death in Rome.

It was a good thing that Paul died an anonymous death. Paul burned really, really bright, for God and for fellow Believers throughout history. Paul's insights still shine with the speed that reaches over centuries. Proverbs 4: 18 talks about the life of a righteous person becoming brighter, as exemplified by the day's sunlight becoming brighter from early morning. Paul did shine brighter as time went on. Some in the Corinthian church were already giving him undue adulation.[339] What did Paul do about such adulation? He nipped it in the bud, killed the idea outright and we never hear of it again. For Paul it is about Jesus and what Jesus accomplished, not Paul. The point is, as Christians, we are indeed to shine brighter as we grow spiritually. Such growth cannot help but advance or polish up our authentic self. However, as people like to say, "It is not about you." Yet, the spiritual side of personal life is about us, otherwise there is no point to salvation. All the same, spirituality as a practice will grow into an actual experience of Christian spiritual brightness, illuminations. The LED (light-emitting diode) flashlight is rated by its lumens. A lumen is the amount of visible light; the number indicates strength and brightness. Christian spiritual brightness is designed,

---

[339] 1 Corinthians 1: 12, 13; 3: 4, 5.

rated, to shine and illumine our spiritual way of being. Occasionally, out spiritual brightness is utilized for extension to illuminate[340] the way for others. Wise caution: some may not initially be open to really bright insights as we perceive sharp ideas to be. The rating of the visible light emitting from each of our lives ultimately depends upon the spiritual insight we take in to put out however. Experience with enlightenment brings familiarity because the familiar with God's involvement can be trusted, beyond what we may presume possible.

---

[340] NCV, Proverbs 27: 17, "As iron sharpens iron, so people can improve [sharpen] each other."

BIBLIOGRAPHY

SOURCE 1

Bloom, Allan, *The Closing of the American Mind*, New York: Simon & Shuster, 1987.

Copleston, Frederick, *A History Of Philosophy*, Vol.4, Garden City: Image Books, 1985.

Grant, David, ed., *Beauties Of Modern British Poetry*, Edinburgh: T. Nelson& Sons, 1871.

Heschel, Abraham, *Man's Search For God*, Santa Fe: Aurora Press, 1998.

Hillman, James, *Re-Visioning Psychology*, New York: Harper Colophon, 1977.

_____, *Healing Fiction*, Dallas: Spring Publications, 1994.

_____, *Kind Of Power*, New York: Currency Doubleday, 1995.

_____, *The Soul's Code*, New York: Random House, 1996.

_____, *The Force of Character*, New York: Random House, 1999.

_____, *City & Soul*, Putnam: Spring Publications, 2006.

Holy Bible, *New Century Version*, Nashville: Thomas Nelson Publishers, 2006.

_____, *English Stand Version*, Wheaton: Crossway, 2011.

Jones, Alan, *Journey Into Christ*, New York: The Seabury Press, 1977.

_____, *Passion For Pilgrimage*, New York: Harper & Row Publishers, 1989.

_____, *Reimagining Christianity*, Hoboken: John Wiley & Sons, 2005.

Koestenbaum, Peter, *The New Image of the Person*, Westport: Greenwood Press, 1978.

Nietzsche, Friedrich, trans., Walter Kaufmann, *The Gay Science*, Vintage Books, 1974.

Novak, Michael, *The Experience of Nothingness*, New York: Harper & Row Publishers, 1970.

Peterson, Eugene, *The Message*, Colorado Springs, Navpress, 1995.

Scott, Walter, "Marmion" stanza XVII, website *allpoetry.com*, anonymously supplied.

Tillich, Paul, *The shaking of the Foundations*, New York: Charles Scribner's Sons, 1948.

_____, *The Courage To Be*, New Heaven: Yale University Press, 1953.

_____, *Systematic Theology*, 3 in 1 volumes, New York: Harper & Row, 1967.

Vincent, Marvin, *Word Studies in the New Testament*, vols. 2, 3, Grand Rapids:

W M B Eerdmans Publishing Company, 1973.

Source 2

Barnhart, Robert, *Dictionary of Etymology*, New York: HarperCollins Publishers, 1995.

Mounce, William, *Mounce's Complete Expository Dictionary of Old & New Testament Words*, Grand Rapids: Zondervan, 2006.

Shipley, Joseph, *Dictionary of Word Origins*, Totowa: Littlefield, Adams & Company, 1967.

Vine, W E, *Vine's Expository Dictionary of New Testament Words*, McLean: MacDonald Publishing Company, 1989.

Index

A

abilities 2, 18, 49–50, 52–53, 56,
58–59, 68, 78–80, 82, 95,
105, 107, 122, 163, 176
acceptance 9, 16, 22, 40, 71, 130–
131, 195
affirmation 25, 60, 130, 139, 166
anchor 99–100
a someone 7, 115, 119–120, 122–
123, 125–126, 130, 132, 163,
165, 171, 196
authenticity 3, 9, 13, 25, 30, 38, 47,
53–54, 84, 129, 145, 153,
155, 162–163, 199–200, 205
authority 38, 43, 51, 53–56, 72, 76,
84, 96, 129, 132, 155, 158,
162, 205

B

Ballast Effect 161
Believer 2–3, 8, 11, 14–15, 18, 20,
22, 26, 30–31, 34, 36, 38,
40–41, 44, 51, 60, 69, 73, 77,
81, 86, 90, 92, 96, 109–110,
112, 120, 123–124, 134–135,
138–139, 142, 147–148, 153,
156, 170, 173, 191, 193–
194, 204
Bible 1–3, 21, 25–26, 36, 65, 87–89,
92, 94–95, 102, 119, 121,
131, 142, 153, 176, 196–198,
203–204, 209
Bloom, Allan 209
bored again 86, 163, 201
burden 12, 39, 85, 131, 148, 150

C

character 10, 17–18, 23, 46–47,
49–50, 54, 56, 61, 72, 80,
83, 93–94, 99–101, 110, 114,
122–123, 133, 143, 154–155,
159, 161, 165, 167–169, 171,
177, 183, 192, 196, 198, 200,
203–204
Christian viii, 1–3, 6, 8–10, 13,
15–17, 19–31, 33–36, 39–40,
42–43, 45, 47, 51–52, 55–56,
59–61, 66, 69, 71–73, 76–77,
79, 81–82, 84, 86, 88, 91,
94–95, 97–100, 104, 107,
110–111, 114–115, 117–118,
120, 123–128, 131, 134, 137,

211

140–141, 147–155, 157, 159,
161–166, 168–170, 175–176,
181, 189–192, 195–196, 198,
200, 203–207

Christian spirituality 1–2, 8, 10,
19–22, 25–27, 30–31, 33, 35,
39–40, 45, 51–52, 60, 71, 73,
77, 82, 84, 97, 99, 104, 108,
111, 114–115, 118, 125, 134,
137, 153–154, 159, 161–162,
164, 175, 181, 196, 198, 200,
203, 206

complete 17, 46, 91, 104, 107–109,
127, 155, 164, 169

conscience 14, 37, 101, 125, 130,
138–139, 160

consciousness 6, 21, 35, 41, 46, 56–
57, 60, 68, 84, 87, 99, 131,
160, 167–169, 174, 202

constant familiarity 46, 55, 58,
62, 154, 166–167, 174, 196,
200, 206

convince 33–34, 54, 133, 199

curiosity 26, 30, 32, 34–35, 52, 69,
91, 117, 160, 174, 181, 192

D

demonic 61, 142, 181, 183–184

destruction 17, 29, 42, 95, 128, 134,
142, 181, 183, 185

devil 6, 135, 156–158

discernment 2, 25–27, 35, 44, 65,
71, 86, 98, 104, 115, 154,
158–160, 163, 171, 174,
189–191

discipline 187, 189–190

F

fall apart 60

fall together 60

forgiveness 7, 11–13, 17, 120, 130,
159, 205

freedom 7, 17, 28–29, 34, 36–37,
40–42, 44–45, 77, 84, 86,
90, 102–103, 108, 120,
130–131, 134–135, 138, 142,
148–150, 152, 154, 160, 165,
177, 180, 184, 195, 203

Friend 77, 92–93, 95–97, 99–
100, 174

fullness 8, 80, 109, 184, 197

future 13, 30, 38, 52, 60, 71, 73, 76,
81, 93, 95, 97–98, 112, 120,
137, 139, 147, 152–155, 157–
158, 168, 171, 193, 202

G

give in 89, 104, 148, 158, 162, 165,
172, 192, 198

God vii–ix, 2–3, 6–9, 12–24,
27–31, 33–35, 37–47, 49–53,
55–56, 59–61, 63, 65–67,
71–72, 78–79, 81, 85–95,
97–105, 107–118, 120–121,
123–135, 137–144, 147–153,
155–159, 164–175, 184–185,
187, 189–198, 203–207, 209

grace 78, 130–131, 134–135, 139–
140, 185, 203

guilt 12, 49, 109, 120, 125, 130–
131, 138, 148–151, 160

H

have-yet 25, 82, 97, 103

heaven 24, 52, 100, 108–109, 141, 202
hell 33–34, 183, 185
Helper 91, 93, 97–99, 174
Heschel, Abraham 209
Hillman, James viii, 53–55, 62, 68, 70, 78, 114, 188, 209
holiness 24, 183, 194, 197
holy 24, 44, 183, 193–196
human nature 1–2, 29, 31, 34, 37, 41, 43, 45, 130, 148–149

I

identity 7, 14, 17–18, 28, 46, 51, 54, 56, 58, 61, 64, 80–81, 99, 101, 103, 105, 107–108, 110, 115, 122–123, 127, 133, 151, 155, 161, 165, 167–169, 192, 196, 205
intellectual astuteness 72, 85–86, 100, 104, 139, 147, 188, 193–195
intellectual bigotry 141, 177–181

J

Jesus 2–3, 10–11, 13, 21, 23–24, 26, 28–32, 34, 37, 39, 42–44, 47, 57, 61, 66, 69, 72, 76–77, 80–81, 88–91, 93–100, 102, 106, 108–109, 116, 120–121, 123–124, 128, 130–132, 135, 137–139, 141, 143, 147–148, 151–153, 156–157, 159, 163, 166, 174–175, 185, 191, 193–195, 203–207
Jones, Alan 209

K

knowledge vii, 7, 9, 19, 25, 27, 42–44, 52, 54, 58, 78, 86, 88, 92, 95, 102, 117, 123, 126–127, 144, 151, 172, 174, 179, 184, 199–200, 206
Koestenbaum, Peter 41–42, 83–84, 149, 154, 210

L

layers 11, 157, 166–168, 180, 196
lonely 21–23
longings 4, 32, 39, 53, 68, 109, 117, 168, 175, 191, 197, 205
love viii, 7, 12, 26–27, 44, 57, 86, 88, 90, 94, 97–98, 109, 113, 118, 123, 131, 133, 151, 158–159, 167, 175–176, 187, 195, 201

N

new self 2, 27–28, 44, 46–47, 55, 60, 66, 72–73, 81, 100, 103, 105, 107, 113, 115, 125, 128, 130, 132, 140, 147, 150, 153, 155, 160, 164–165, 168–169, 187, 191–192, 194, 196–197, 205
Nietzsche, Friedrich 210
Novak, Michael 69–70, 72, 210

O

old self 28, 44, 47, 60, 81, 103, 105, 107, 115, 117, 125, 128, 132, 147, 153, 165, 167–168, 187, 192, 194, 197
openness 178

P

paraword 98–99, 103, 113, 122–123, 156, 159, 161
past 7, 13–14, 16, 22, 24, 28–29, 36, 40–41, 45, 63, 69, 71, 81, 95, 110, 120, 124, 152, 154–155, 164–165, 201, 205
peace 2, 8, 11, 26, 28, 32, 35, 39, 90, 100, 137, 139, 147–149, 166, 182, 187, 190, 205
personality 2–3, 9, 14, 16–18, 21–23, 30, 37, 42, 46–47, 49–62, 64, 66–68, 70, 78–80, 92, 95, 97, 99–101, 103, 105, 107, 111, 122, 128, 132, 143, 147–148, 152, 154–155, 160–161, 163, 165, 167–168, 172, 176, 184, 192–193, 196, 205
plateau experience 85–86, 166
presence 9, 23, 25, 51, 55, 60–61, 64, 67, 70, 90, 96, 98, 101, 111, 115–116, 149, 155, 157, 163, 166, 168, 174, 192–193, 200–201, 203–204
process 7, 14–15, 21, 23, 34, 40, 56, 60–61, 66, 95, 102, 115, 117–118, 122, 127, 135, 142, 144–145, 147–148, 155, 161, 164–165, 168, 172, 179, 181, 189, 192–194, 198, 204

Q

questioning experience 69–70, 85, 180
questions 4, 16, 35–36, 69–70, 111, 113, 129, 142, 163, 191

R

reason's power 19, 127, 174, 177–178, 180
relaxed 26, 28, 35, 79, 82–84, 87, 90, 104, 129, 135, 140, 148, 162, 203
renovation 169, 171, 198
rest 20, 26, 39, 90, 147–148, 160
rightwise 122, 128, 158, 171, 206
rules rule 60, 85, 87, 184, 190, 201

S

salvation 2, 7, 13–15, 17–21, 26, 29, 31, 37–38, 40, 43, 45–46, 55, 57, 60–61, 66, 72, 81, 95, 97, 104, 117, 120–122, 124, 127, 130, 132, 137–142, 147, 154–155, 164–166, 168–169, 187, 191, 193–196, 199, 203–205, 207
sanctification 21, 23–24, 40, 57, 60–61, 122, 124, 127, 132, 147, 161, 164–165, 187, 192–195, 197–198, 204
Savior 3, 26, 37, 76–77, 93–95, 99–100, 137, 174
self-esteem 79, 81, 97, 111, 113
Shepherd 72, 76–78, 93, 96, 98, 114
sin less 24, 134, 148, 156, 194
soul vii, viii, 2, 7, 9, 14–18, 21, 25–26, 29, 32–33, 35–36, 40, 42, 45–46, 54–57, 61–63, 65–72, 75–81, 86, 88–90, 92, 95, 97, 100–101, 103–105, 110–111, 114–116, 119, 125, 129, 133, 143–144, 149, 151, 155, 160–164, 166–171, 173–174, 176–177, 179, 182,

185, 188, 192–193, 197–203, 205–206

soul-making 61, 64–65, 67–69, 72, 75, 77–78, 80, 86, 92, 95, 97, 103, 105, 115, 129, 144, 152, 155, 161–164, 166–168, 170–171, 177, 192, 197–198, 205

Spirit 9, 17, 22, 24, 28, 34, 38, 50, 59, 65–66, 78, 89, 91, 93, 95, 98, 101, 104, 115, 117, 122, 128, 132, 135, 137, 139–140, 156, 169–170, 184, 192, 194–195, 204

Spiritual growth 3, 5, 15, 21, 117, 165

stand out 79, 81, 119, 153, 164–165, 168

style 2, 4, 21, 24, 30, 42, 51, 57, 99–100, 109, 134, 137–138, 147, 160–165, 175, 192–193, 196–197, 200–201, 203–206

T

temptation 132–135, 139, 143, 155–158, 169–170

terrorism 178

Tillich, Paul 210

U

understanding 3, 7–8, 19, 26–27, 31, 59, 77, 86, 88, 95, 102, 120, 122, 151, 159, 165, 167, 171–172, 179, 196, 203, 206

V

Vincent, Marvin 210

violence 128, 177, 180–182

W

wisdom viii, 7–8, 19, 25–27, 40, 44, 54, 59, 65, 68, 75, 79, 82–84, 86–87, 98, 115–116, 129, 135, 154, 156–160, 162–163, 166–167, 169–170, 172, 180, 182, 188, 195, 198–200, 202, 205

About the Author

Bruce Metzger, 65, is not a university teacher nor a minister. Metzger is involved in Bible studies at Coquitlam Presbyterian Church. Camille his wife, live in Coquitlam a suburb of Vancouver. Metzger has attended Bible College, 3 year program, associated with the Pentecostal denomination, and, 2 years of philosophy at university. Then practical life with irksome difficulties got in the way. He has continued to read further, to understand God and human nature. May contact at Facebook or Twitter.

For 35 years Bruce has been driving truck, mostly 22 wheeler. "I discovered I'm a natural driving trucks with big wheels, and as a driver, by fortuitous conditions," said with pleasure, "because of delay times, I can read books and while driving listen to aubiobooks, on the job." Metzger adds, "God saved me a second time from being a boring pedantic intellectual. I'm also trusted to deliver people's material objects, which become commodities that improves yet other's lives." Bruce also trusts to "transfer" helpful ideas that can encourage spiritual growth, while sitting on little wheels, writing.

CPSIA information can be obtained
at www.ICGtesting.com
Printed in the USA
LVOW03s0522290318
571537LV00001B/1/P